Hearts and Minds

An Afterschool Program for Developing Reading Literacy and Emotional Intelligence

Susanna Palomares • Patricia Rowland • Kelly Rowland

Cover: Dave Cowan

Copyright © 2012 by Innerchoice Publishing • All rights reserved

ISBN - 10: 1-56499-084-6

ISBN - 13: 978-1-56499-084-6

INNERCHOICE Publishing
15079 Oak Chase Court
Wellington, FL 33414

www.InnerchoicePublishing.com

Activity sheets may be reproduced in quantities sufficient for distribution to children in programs utilizing *Hearts and Minds*. All other reproduction, in any manner or for any purpose whatsoever, is explicitly prohibited without written permission. Request for such permission should be directed to INNERCHOICE PUBLISHING.

Contents

Introduction 1

Design of the Book 3

The Importance of Emotional Intelligence. 6

The Value of Sharing Circles 8

Sharing Circle Rules 11

How to Lead a Sharing Circle 12

More About Sharing Circle Steps and Rules 17

Tips to Help Develop Reading Literacy .22

Tips to Optimize Learning and Engagement 23

Thematic Units

RESPECT 26

KINDNESS 42

TOLERANCE 62

SERVICE TO OTHERS 82

RESPONSIBILITY 96

SELF-CONTROL 116

PEER PRESSURE 136

Introduction

Reading, writing, speaking, and listening are all interwoven processes, and each helps build and strengthen the other. Through its variety of activities, Hearts and Minds fosters the relationship between these four necessary skills while helping to fully develop each. Hearts and Minds provides multiple opportunities for children to read and listen to stories, to listen and respond to verbal directions, and to read and write on their personal Experience Sheets. They get to create their own stories and write about their own lives. The Sharing Circle provides the opportunity for the children to share their ideas verbally, which is the prime method for developing oral language skills. Listening to others share their thoughts helps develop effective listening skills. Through all this sharing and listening the children are learning the conventions of conversation and appropriate listening and speaking behavior. Through the Sharing Circles the children learn to clearly express their thoughts and feelings so others can understand.

Hearts and Minds also directly affects the social and emotional development of children in a number of ways. Each unit has a social-emotional character theme that is fully developed and explored through the stories, activities, and Sharing Circles. As the children are actively engaged in talking, sharing, listening and cooperatively doing, they are learning important skills for getting along with others. Discussions and self-reflection encourage self-awareness and self-knowledge. By following rules of good communication in the Sharing Circle and other activities, the children get to express their thoughts, feelings and ideas and to learn to be respectful of, and appreciate, the ideas and feelings of others.

Through its integration of language development and social-emotional learning, Hearts and Minds is designed to help children grow into capable and caring young people

Design of the Book

The Stories

The first component of each unit is a short story that embodies the unit theme. Depending on the reading levels of your children and your preferences, these stories may be read aloud to the children or duplicated and distributed for individual reading or small group read-arounds. Possible new vocabulary words are listed on the first page of each unit, as well. A good way to introduce these words to the children is to write them on the board and then briefly discuss each word. Ask the children if they are familiar with the word, and if they know what it means. Share the definitions with the children and ask them to listen for each word in the story.

Several discussion questions follow each story. Use these to facilitate an exchange of reactions to the story, examination of the dilemmas and choices faced by characters in the story, and the meaning of the story in general. Always review the questions in advance and adjust them to suit the readiness of your children to deal with various concepts.

Also following each story is an "Experience Sheet," which you may duplicate and distribute to your children, giving them an opportunity to respond personally to the story and to write about similar situations that they have faced in their own lives. Allow the children to share their answers to the questions in small groups. This is an excellent way to help the children further internalize the concepts presented in the story and unit as a whole.

The Activities

Each unit also includes two engaging group activities. These activities provide a wide range of experiences from art, to role-play, to games and are designed to help the children internalize the values inherent in the theme of each unit.

At the conclusion of every activity, you'll find another list of "Discussion Questions." These discussion questions are provided to help you involve the children in thinking about and summarizing the learnings derived from that particular activity. They promote thoughtful reasoning, the use of higher-level thinking skills, and internalization of knowledge and skills. Use any or all of the discussion questions provided, and feel free to ask your own questions. When planning, always allow plenty of time for discussion during and at the end of the activity.

Feel free to adapt the activities to suit the ages, ability levels, cultural/ethnic backgrounds, and interests of your children.

The Sharing Circles

The Sharing Circle is an extremely powerful process for the development of empathy, effective listening, self-control, and many other social and emotional learning skills. Part of its value for this purpose lies in the fact that it is guided by a clear procedure, rules, and a specific topic. In addition, the process requires that children demonstrate respect, responsibility, trust, caring, and fairness as a condition of participating in every circle.

Oral language development is also an area of focus in the Sharing Circle. As the key mode of expression in each Sharing Circle, oral language is engaged in with enthusiasm because the children are encouraged to express themselves and talk about their own experiences and feelings while others listen respectfully without interruption. In this way the development of oral language is strengthened and refined through its use. Furthermore, we believe oral language is a key which unlocks the door to literacy. One of the most exciting aspects of oral language is its power to stimulate other forms of expression. Children readily engage in reading, writing, acting, playing games and singing when they can read, draw, dramatize, play, and sing about things they choose to talk about first, and vice versa. In this way the Sharing Circle supports the integration of the language arts.

The Reflection Page

At the conclusion of the activities in each unit, you'll find an exercise entitled "What Did You Learn?" These exercises comprise a very important repeating element of Hearts and Minds. Reflection is an important part of learning, and these reflection pages encourage the children to look back on, think about, and learn from what they have experienced in each unit. Learning brains need this time for reflection, consolidation and integration. Reflection helps develop critical thinking skills and integrates both emotional and intellectual growth. To illicit the deepest meaning allow the children to be creative and find their own way to express their thoughts and learning. Writing, drawing, scribbles, poetry, simple notes, etc. are all valuable.

When the children have completed their reflection, be sure that they have an opportunity to share their pages and tell others what they have learned. Through the process of making their thinking visible on the page and then articulating to others what they learned, they are strengthening learning pathways in the brain and committing this learning to long-term memory

The Parent Letter

Provided for you are parent letters that are to go home with each child upon the conclusion of the first day a new unit is introduced and the story has been read. Building a bridge between home and afterschool is a key ingredient of children's success in all areas, especially with developing emotional intelligence.

The parent letters are designed to give parents a synopsis of the story and some background knowledge of the theme of each unit. We have included questions for the parents to ask their child to promote discussion at home, along with tips they can use at home so that the concepts of each theme are reinforced.

The Importance of Emotional Intelligence

Social and emotional learning (SEL) is a broad set of skills and competencies that, when acquired, lead to the development of emotional intelligence. Just as we want children to demonstrate intelligence in academic areas, we also want them to be intelligent when they relate to others and in understanding themselves.

Children who have high levels of emotional intelligence— who manage their own feelings well, and who recognize and respond effectively to the feelings of others — are at an advantage in every area of life, whether family and peer relationships, school, sports, or community and organizational pursuits. Children with well-developed social and emotional skills are also more likely to lead happy and productive lives, and to master the habits of mind that will assure them personal and career success as adults.

When emotional intelligence is nurtured with the same concern as IQ, young people tolerate frustration better, get into fewer fights, and engage in less self-destructive behavior. They are healthier, less lonely, less impulsive, and more focused. Human relationships improve, and so does academic achievement.

Being able to effectively manage an interpersonal conflict is one example of a social skill or intelligence. Being able to demonstrate self-control when provoked and angry is an example of an emotional skill or intelligence. When children are able to use these types of social and emotional skills in their daily lives, they are demonstrating emotional intelligence.

Social and emotional competencies have often been a "hidden" agenda in many afterschool programs and regular classrooms. These skills are recognized as important but often not explicitly taught. However, with an accumulating abundance of research and direct observation, these social and emotional competencies are more and more being recognized as crucial to success in all aspects of 21st century life. School work, adult work, relationships, and general wellbeing are all dependent on having skills in such areas as self-control, goal-setting, active listening, respect for others, tolerance, and conflict and anger management. Children (and adults) lacking skills such as these struggle to perform academically and to get along with others. Conversely, children with well developed social and emotional skills, or emotional intelligence, perform better in school, get along better with peers, and more effectively manage the inevitable challenges and setbacks of life.

Hearts and Minds provides dozens of easy-to-implement and engaging activities, stories, and Sharing Circles designed to build understanding and skills in each of the following key areas of social and emotional learning:

- Kindness
- Tolerance
- Self-Control
- Respect for Self and Others
- Peer Pressure
- Responsibility
- Service to others

By purposefully integrating social and emotional learning into your afterschool activities, you are helping your children develop the emotional intelligence to be more effective in all areas of their lives both today and beyond.

The Value of Sharing Circles

A safe, supportive and caring afterschool program is something that parents and children want and appreciate and that the afterschool staff values and strives to create. Because Sharing Circles provide a simple, easy-to-do process for developing positive relationships between teachers and children and among the children, it is a prime means for fostering respect and rapport and creating an emotionally safe place while enhancing the development of critical social skills.

The Sharing Circle is a small-group discussion process in which the children and adult leader share their feelings, experiences, and insights in response to specific, assigned topics. In a Sharing Circle everyone is expected to follow the rules that promote good communication while assuring cooperation, trust, and confidentiality.

The personal traits and social skills needed to grow into an effective, self-actualized person develop largely within a social environment. The nature of the Sharing Circle environment — the messages it sends to children and the behaviors it encourages and discourages are highly conducive to their development. Children follow clear rules of conduct, accept ownership of those rules, are supportive of one another, and experience a sense of satisfaction by complying with the guidelines and procedures of the circle.

The Sharing Circle is an ideal way to incorporate social and emotional learning into an afterschool program on a regular basis. It's structure and process provide the foundational building blocks of emotional learning. First, the Sharing Circle process provides emotional safety, security, unconditional acceptance, and nurturing to each child. Second, the topics are stimulating in their ability to provoke self-inquiry and address real-life experiences and issues and the full range of emotions associated with them. Third, the ambiance created through regular use of the Sharing Circle creates close, yet respectful, relationship leading to high levels of group cohesiveness and creativity. And finally, the immediacy of the Sharing Circle ensures that every child's contributions are heard and accepted on the spot. The attentiveness of other Circle members (children and adult leader) along with their verbal and non-verbal positive reactions constitute a powerful form of immediate and affirming feedback.

Skill Development

The process, rules and topics of the Sharing Circle help facilitate the social and emotional growth of children in a number of significant ways. As children follow the rules and relate to each other verbally during the Sharing Circle, they are practicing respectful listening and oral communication. By listening patiently and respectfully to others taking their turns, they are learning the important master skill of self-control. As they listen carefully while other children ponder and discuss the various topics, the children have repeated opportunities to mentally take the perspectives of others. By sharing their own experiences, thoughts, and ideas, they are gaining awareness and control over their own feelings, thoughts and behaviors.

The Sharing Circle topics offered in this book address many skills, such as keeping agreements, developing responsible habits, solving problems, demonstrating respect for self and others, being loyal, being trustworthy and honest, following rules, demonstrating kindness and consideration, and resolving conflicts, etc.

Topics like these help identify core ethical values, and require children to describe incidents and behaviors from their own experience that illustrate those values. In this way Sharing Circle topics are all connecting to what children already know.

The Sharing Circle allows children to confront difficult decision-making situations. In response to the topics posed, children are asked to state positions, to think about their reasons for selecting those positions, and to listen to the positions and reasoning of others.

Learning to Get Along

As children learn to relate effectively to others, issues related to acceptable and unacceptable behavior surface again and again. Children learn that all people have the power to influence one another. They become aware not only of how others affect them, but of the effects their behaviors have on others.

The Sharing Circle has been designed so that healthy, responsible behaviors are modeled by the adult leader in his or her role as circle leader. Also, the rules require that the children relate responsibly and effectively to one another. The Sharing Circle brings out and affirms the positive qualities inherent in everyone and encourages the children to practice effective modes of communication. Being a place where everyone is listened to, their feelings accepted, and their contributions judged as having value, the Sharing Circle teaches cooperation and promotes caring. All Sharing Circles are guided by a spirit of collaborations and trust. When children practice fair, respectful interactions with one another, they benefit from the experience and are likely to employ those responsible behaviors in other life situations.

Sharing Circle Rules

- Everyone gets a turn to share, including the leader.

- You can skip your turn if you wish.

- Listen to the person who is sharing.

- There are no interruptions, probing, put-downs, or gossip.

- Share the time equally.

How to Lead a Sharing Circle

This section is a thorough guide for conducting Sharing Circles. It covers major points to keep in mind and answers questions which will arise as you lead Sharing Circles with children. Please remember that these guidelines are presented to assist you, not to restrict you. Follow them, and trust your own leadership style at the same time.

The Sharing Circle is a structured communication process that provides children a safe place for learning about life, enhancing oral-language skills and developing important aspects of social-emotional learning.

First, we'll provide a brief overview of the process of leading a Sharing Circle and then we'll cover each step in more detail.

A Sharing Circle begins when a group of children and the adult leader sit down together in a circle so that each person is able to see the others easily. The leader of the Sharing Circle briefly greets and welcomes each child, conveying a feeling of enthusiasm blended with seriousness.

When everyone appears comfortable, the leader takes a few moments to review the Sharing Circle Rules. These rules inform the children of the positive behaviors required of them and guarantees the emotional safety and security, and equality of each member.

After the children understand and agree to follow the rules, the leader announces the topic for the session. A brief elaboration of the topic follows in which the leader provides examples and possibly mentions the topics relationship to prior topics or to other things the children are involved in. Then the leader re-states the topic and allows a little silence during which circle members may review and ponder their own related memories and mentally prepare their verbal response to the topic. (The topics and elaborations are provided in this book.)

Next, the leader invites the children to voluntarily share their responses to the topic, one at a time. No one is forced to share, but everyone is given an opportunity to share while all the other circle members listen attentively. The circle participants tell the group about themselves, their personal experiences, thoughts, feelings, hopes and dreams as they relate to the topic. Most of the circle time is devoted to this sharing phase because of its central importance.

During this time, the leader assumes a dual role—that of leader and participant. The leader makes sure that everyone who wishes to speak is given the opportunity while simultaneously enforcing the rules as necessary. The leader also takes a turn to speak if he or she wishes.

After everyone who wants to share has done so, the leader introduces the next phase of the Sharing Circle by asking several discussion questions. This phase represents a transition to the intellectual mode and allows participants to reflect on and express learnings gained from the sharing phase. It's in this phase that participants are able to crystallize learnings and to understand the relevance of the discussion to their daily lives. (Discussion questions for each topic are provided in this book.)

When the children have finished discussing their responses to the questions and the session has reached a natural closure, the leader ends the session. The leader thanks the children for being part of the Sharing Circle and states that it is over.

What follows is a more detailed look at the process of leading a Sharing Circle.

Steps for Leading a Sharing Circle
1. Welcome Sharing Circle members
2. Review the Sharing Circle rules *
3. Introduce the topic
4. Sharing by circle members
5. Ask discussion questions
6. Close the circle

*optional after the first few sessions

1. Welcome Sharing Circle members

As you sit down with the children in a Sharing Circle group, remember that you are not teaching a lesson. You are facilitating a group of children. Establish a positive atmosphere. In a relaxed manner, address each child by name, using eye contact and conveying warmth. An attitude of seriousness blended with enthusiasm will let the children know that this Sharing Circle group is an important learning experience—an activity that can be interesting and meaningful.

2. Review the Sharing Circle rules

At the beginning of the first Sharing Circle, and at appropriate intervals thereafter, go over the rules for the circle. They are:

Sharing Circle Rules
- Everyone gets a turn to share, including the leader.
- You can skip your turn if you wish.
- Listen to the person who is sharing.
- There are no interruptions, probing, put-downs, or gossip.
- Share the time equally.

From this point on, demonstrate to the children that you expect them to remember and abide by the ground rules. Convey that you think well of them and know they are fully capable of responsible behavior. Let them know that by coming to the Sharing Circle they are making a commitment to listen and show acceptance and respect for the other children and you. It is helpful to write the rules on chart paper and keep them on display for the benefit of each Sharing Circle session.

3. Introduce the topic

State the topic, and then in your own words, elaborate and provide examples as each lesson in this book suggests. The introduction or elaboration of the topic is designed to get children focused and thinking about how they will respond to the topic. By providing more than just the mere statement of the topic, the elaboration gives children a few moments to expand their thinking and to make a personal connection to the topic at hand. Add clarifying statements of your own that will help the children understand the topic. Answer questions about the topic, and emphasize that there are no "wrong" responses. Finally, restate the topic, opening the session to responses (theirs and yours). Sometimes taking your turn first helps the children understand the aim of the topic. The introductions, as written in this book, are provided to give you some general ideas for opening the Sharing Circle. You should state the introduction in your own words and not read verbatum out of the book. Feel free to adjust and modify the introduction and elaboration to suit the ages, abilities, levels, cultural/ethnic backgrounds and interests of your children.

4. Sharing by circle members

The most important point to remember is this: The purpose of these Sharing Circles is to give children an opportunity to express themselves and be accepted for the experiences, thoughts, and feelings they share. Avoid taking the action away from the children. They are the stars!

5. Ask discussion questions

Responding to discussion questions is the cognitive portion of the process. During this phase, the leader asks thought-provoking questions to stimulate free discussion and higher-level thinking. Each Sharing Circle lesson in this book concludes with several discussion questions. At times, you may want to formulate questions that are more appropriate to the level of understanding in your children—or to what was actually shared in the circle.

6. Close the circle

The ideal time to end a Sharing Circle is when the discussion question phase reaches natural closure. Sincerely thank everyone for being part of the circle. Don't thank specific children for speaking, as doing so might convey the impression that speaking is more appreciated than just listening. Then close the group by saying, "This Sharing Circle is over," or "OK, that ends our circle."

More About Sharing Circle Steps and Rules

The next few paragraphs offer further clarification concerning leadership of Sharing Circles.

Who gets to talk? Everyone. The importance of acceptance cannot be overly stressed. In one way or another practically every ground rule says one thing: accept one another. When you model acceptance of children, they will learn how to be accepting. Each individual in the group is important and deserves a turn to speak if he or she wishes to take it. Equal opportunity to become involved should be given to everyone in the Sharing Circle.

Members should be reinforced equally for their contributions. There are many reasons why a leader may become more enthused over what one child shares than another. The response may be more on target, reflect more depth, be more entertaining, be philosophically more in keeping with one's own point of view, and so on. However, children need to be given equal recognition for their contributions, even if the contribution is to listen silently throughout the session.

In most of the Sharing Circles, plan to take a turn and address the topic, too. Children usually appreciate it very much and learn a great deal when their teachers, and other adults are willing to tell about their own experiences, thoughts, and feelings. In this way you let your children know that you acknowledge your own humanness.

Does everyone have to take a turn? No. Children may choose to skip their turns. If the circle becomes a pressure situation in which the members are coerced in any way to speak, it will become an unsafe place where participants are not comfortable. Meaningful discussion is unlikely in such an atmosphere. By allowing children to make this choice, you are showing them that you accept their right to remain silent if that is what they choose to do.

As you begin the circle, it's important to remember that it's not a problem if one or more children decline to speak. If you are imperturbable and accepting when this happens, you let them know you are offering them an opportunity to experience something you think is valuable. You as a leader should not feel compelled to share a personal experience in every session, either. However, if you decline to speak in most of the sessions, this may have an inhibiting effect on the children' willingness to share.

Some leaders ask the participants to raise their hands when they wish to speak, while others simply allow free verbal sharing without soliciting the leader's permission first. Choose the procedure that works best for you. And do not merely go around the circle.

Sometimes a silence occurs during a session. Don't feel you have to jump in every time someone stops talking. During silences children have an opportunity to think about what they would like to share or to contemplate an important idea they've heard. A general rule of thumb is to allow silence to the point that you observe group discomfort. At that point move on. Do not switch to another topic. To do so implies you will not be satisfied until the children speak. If you change to another topic, you are telling them you didn't really mean it when you said they didn't have to take a turn if they didn't want to.

How can I encourage effective listening? The Sharing Circle is a time (and place) for children and leaders to strengthen the habit of listening by doing it over and over again. No one was born knowing how to listen effectively to others. It is a skill like any other that gets better as it is practiced. In the immediacy of the Sharing Circle the members become keenly aware of the necessity to listen, and most children respond by expecting it of one another.

In these Sharing Circles, listening is defined as the respectful focusing of attention on individual speakers. It includes eye contact with the speaker and open body posture. It doesn't allow interruptions of any kind. When you lead a circle, listen and encourage listening in the children by (1) focusing your attention on the person who is speaking, (2) being receptive to what the speaker is saying (not mentally planning your next remark), and (3) recognizing the speaker when she finishes speaking, either verbally ("Thanks, Shirley") or nonverbally (a nod and a smile).

To encourage effective listening in the children, reinforce them by letting them know you have noticed they were listening to each other and you appreciate it.

How can I ensure the children get equal time? When group members share the time equally, they demonstrate their acceptance of the notion that everyone's contribution is of equal importance. It is not uncommon to have at least one dominator in a group. This person is usually totally unaware that by continuing to talk he or she is taking time from others who are less assertive. An important social skill is knowing how you affect others in a group and when dominating a group is inappropriate behavior.

Be very clear with the children about the purpose of this ground rule. Tell them at the outset how much time there is. When it is your turn, always limit your own contribution. If someone goes on and on, do intervene (dominators need to know what they are doing), but do so as gently and respectfully as you can.

What are some examples of put-downs? Put-downs convey the message, "You are not okay as you are." Some put-downs are deliberate, but many are made unknowingly. Both kinds are undesirable in a Sharing Circle because they destroy the atmosphere of acceptance and disrupt the flow of sharing and discussion. Typical put-downs include:
- over questioning.
- statements that have the effect of teaching or preaching
- advice giving
- one-upsmanship

- criticism, disapproval, or objections
- sarcasm
- statements or questions of disbelief

How can I deal with put-downs? There are two major ways for dealing with put-downs: preventing them from occurring and intervening when they do.

Going over the rules with the children at the beginning of each Sharing Circle, particularly in the earliest sessions, is a helpful preventive technique. Another is to reinforce the children when they adhere to the rule. Be sure to use non patronizing, non evaluative language.

Unacceptable behavior should be stopped the moment it is recognized by the leader. When you become aware that a put-down is occurring, do whatever you ordinarily do to stop destructive behavior. If one child gives another an unasked-for bit of advice, say for example, "Jane, please give Alicia a chance to tell her story." To a child who interrupts say, "Ed, it's Jose's turn." In most cases the fewer words, the better—children automatically tune out messages delivered as lectures.

Sometimes children disrupt the group by starting a private conversation with the person next to them. Touch the offender on the arm or shoulder while continuing to give eye contact to the child who is speaking. If you can't reach the offender, simply remind him or her of the rule about listening.

If children persist in putting others down or disrupt the circle, ask to see them at another time and hold a brief one-to-one conference, urging them to follow the rules. Suggest that they reconsider their membership in the group. Make it clear that if they don't intend to honor the rules, they are not to come to the group.

How can I keep children from gossiping? Periodically remind children that using names and sharing embarrassing information in a Sharing Circle is not acceptable. Urge the children to relate personally to one another, but not to tell intimate details of their lives.

What should the leader do during the discussion question phase?
Conduct this part of the process as an open forum, giving children the opportunity to discuss a variety of ideas and accept those that make sense to them. Don't impose your opinions on the children, or allow the children to impose theirs on one another. Ask open-ended questions, encourage higher-level thinking, contribute your own ideas when appropriate, and act as a facilitator.

In Conclusion: The Two Most Important Things to Remember

No matter what happens in a Sharing Circle session, the following two elements are the most critical:

1. Everyone gets a turn.
2. Everyone who takes a turn gets listened to with respect.

What does it mean to get a turn? Imagine a pie divided into as many pieces as there are people in the group. Telling the children that everyone gets a turn, whether they want to take it or not, is like telling them that each one gets a piece of the pie. Some children may not want their piece right away, but they know it's there to take when they do want it. As the Sharing Circle leader, you must protect this shared ownership. Getting a turn not only represents a chance to talk, it is an assurance that every member of the group has a "space" that no one else will violate.

When children take their turn, they will be listened to. There will be no attempt by anyone to manipulate what a child is offering. That is, the child will not be probed, interrupted, interpreted, analyzed, put-down, joked-at, advised, preached to, and so on. To "listen to" is to respectfully focus attention on the speaker and to let the speaker know that you have heard what he or she has said.

In the final analysis, the only way that a Sharing Circle can be evaluated is against these two criteria. Thus, if only two children choose to speak, but are listened to—even if they don't say very "deep" or "meaningful" things—the Sharing Circle can be considered a success.

Tips to Help Develop Reading Literacy

Have Books Available

Provide books that the children can comfortably read. When children read accurately and understand what they are reading, their chances of reading success increase significantly, and obviously makes reading much more enjoyable. Besides educating, books should also entertain. Make sure books are available that the children want to read just for pure pleasure of doing so. Provide books that cover a wide range of topics. Encourage the children to read and re-read favorite books. These repeated readings improve children's fluency and comprehension. Allow the children to read and discuss what they are reading in pairs and small groups.

Read to the Children Often

Read to the children often – everyday, if you can. You'll model fluent reading as you read and re-read books to them. Even though they may be able to read on their own, it's important to find time to read books and stories that the children enjoy. This helps them learn vocabulary and pronunciation while they listen to examples of fluent reading.

Make Reading Active

Use readers' theatre to promote reading. Have children "act out" stories that they read or hear. Creating scripts, designing costumes, and staging make a story interactive and can really bring all dimensions of reading literacy alive.

Tips to Optimize Learning and Engagement

Safety First

When children feel stress and are anxious and fearful, it's hard for them to settle down and learn or get engaged in positive pro-social activities. Although you aren't in a position to overcome problems in a child's life, you can make sure that your afterschool program is a safe, caring, and welcoming place where everyone is treated with respect and bully behavior is not tolerated. Positive relationships and rapport are key elements in creating an atmosphere of safety and security. Do things like greeting children when they arrive. Make sure they know you care and are glad to see them. Be sure each child gets some form of personal acknowledgment and attention each day.

Activate Prior Knowledge

The latest research into how the human brain learns is showing that it is essential to use children's life experiences, prior knowledge, and memories as a foundation upon which new learnings are built. In order for a new learning to be retained it has to connect to something the child already has some experience with. Asking questions to get the children thinking about what they already know about the topic you will be teaching is an important way to bring personal relevance and meaning to the topic. At the beginning of any activity, or story, ask questions that will help the children recall and identify what they already now about the topic. For example, if you are beginning the "Service to Others" unit before you read the story ask the children to think about a time they helped someone out. When beginning the "Kindness" unit, you could ask the children to recall kind acts that others have done for them.

When introducing each Sharing Circle Topic to the children, you will be providing an elaboration that naturally helps each child to personally relate the topic to his or her life experiences. These topic elaborations are provided in each Sharing Circle you'll find in Hearts and Minds.

Tap Into Feelings

Everything the human brain learns is filtered through emotions. Emotion is the gate-keeper to learning. Learning and emotion are so intertwined that they constantly influence each other. Learning takes place easily when it is attached to strong feelings. Learning is enhanced when the activities, Sharing Circles, and stories are presented and performed in a joyous, fun, and exciting fashion. Laughter, group interaction, and just plain fun are good for learning, lowering stress, and making your afterschool program a place where children want to be.

All the activities presented in Hearts and Minds are designed to promote learning and involvement by being fun and engaging experiences for the children, and you.

THEMATIC UNITS

RESPECT

— Respect children because they're human beings and they deserve respect, and they'll grow up to be better people.

Benjamin Spock

— If one doesn't respect oneself, one can have neither love nor respect for others.

Ayn Rand

Vocabulary Words

- Ignored
- Humiliated
- Anxious
- Courteous
- Avoiding
- Amazing

How the Turkey Became a Star

by Tom Pettepiece

Todd was a turkey. But not all the time. Sometimes he was a squirrel and other times he was just a weird stupid jerk.

At least Ralph thought so, because that's what Ralph called Todd every time he saw him. Ralph was a bully.

One day Todd was walking with Nathan on his way to class, when Ralph, who was about a foot taller than Todd, deliberately bumped Todd, as he passed. Everybody saw that Ralph did it on purpose.

"Hey Punk," he said meanly. "Watch where you're going."

Todd tried to ignore him and kept on walking.

"Hey Stupid! Stop when I'm talking to you."

Todd stopped and looked at Nathan. He was scared. Ralph came over and hit Todd on the shoulder as hard as he could. By now, everyone was looking at Todd. He tried, but couldn't hold back the tears. It hurt and worse then that, he felt helpless, alone and humiliated.

"You little wimp," Ralph said. "Look at the crybaby. Crybaby!"

The bell rang. Todd would be late, and everyone would notice he'd been crying.

This sort of thing was common. Every day Ralph did something to Todd. He would sit behind Todd during reading and poke him in the back with a pencil. He'd grab his lunch bag and empty it into the trash while everyone watched.

Occasionally, Todd would say, "Knock it off, Ralph" or "Leave me alone!" but this only seemed to make Ralph more keen to pick on Todd.

The only thing that worked was to stay out of Ralph's way. Todd would plan the time he got to school to miss Ralph before class. At lunch, he'd walk clear around the playground so Ralph couldn't find him.

In short, Todd spent most of his time at school avoiding Ralph. As a result, he made few other friends, was accused of daydreaming by the teacher, missed assignments, and sometimes got poor grades. Ralph was running Todd's life. The only thing that made life bearable was thinking about summer.

That summer Todd spent several weeks at camp. He created computer games. He learned to spell backwards as fast as he could frontwards. He swam and hiked, and he painted colorful pictures of horses and houses. He sang, acted in skits, and spoke in front of the group. He even learned how to make himself seem heavy or light to pick up, just by picturing in his mind he was an anchor or a feather.

Todd learned that his brain could do amazing things. For the summer, Todd was happy. He felt good about himself and made lots of new friends. The camp was called "Starshine" and Todd was indeed a star!

The day before school started, Todd's mother asked how Todd thought school would be this year. Todd felt anxious. He was already worried about Ralph. But Todd's mother said, "You're a star, Todd. You don't need Ralph calling you names or bothering you again. You're too bright and too confident for that!"

Todd thought about what his mother said, and thought back to all the things he had learned over the summer. He realized that he was strong and capable. He knew that now he had control over how he thought and reacted to things, and that Ralph wasn't going to be able to bully him anymore.

Ralph was there the first day of school, and looked meanly at Todd when they passed in the hallway. But before he could say anything, Todd stopped, smiled confidently and said, "Ralph, don't start anything, because it won't work. You don't have to like me, but it is time you started showing me some respect."

Ralph took a step backwards. He sensed immediately that Todd had changed, and it threw him completely. Ralph mumbled and growled and shuffled his feet, but he couldn't think of anything to say.

Todd stood his ground for a full minute. Finally he said cheerfully, "See ya around, Ralph," and walked away.

Ralph didn't know a lot about respect. Most of what he did know, he had learned the hard way. It took him a long time to understand what he had learned from Todd that day. Though, just to be safe, he steered clear of Todd while he was figuring it out.

Eventually Ralph learned that being courteous and respectful toward people got him all the attention he needed, without the need to constantly prove that he was bigger or tougher than everyone else. He even learned to be friendly.

Four or five years later, when Ralph's bully streak had completely faded away, Todd and Ralph became good friends.

Discussion Questions:

1. How did Ralph's bullying behavior affect Todd?
2. Why didn't Ralph show respect for Todd in the beginning?
3. Do you think Ralph respected himself? Why or why not?
4. What is respectful behavior?
5. Does everyone deserve respect, or is respect something that must be earned?
6. When you loose respect for someone, does that mean that you can treat the person badly? Why or why not?

How the Turkey Became a Star

Experience Sheet

Think about the story of Todd and Ralph. What did you learn from the story? Read and answer the following questions. Be prepared to talk about your answers with a partner or to the group.

1. What did Todd learn about himself at camp?

2. What did Todd do that helped to change Ralph's attitude toward him?

3. What does it mean to respect someone?

4. How do you show respect for others?

How We Show Respect
Interviews, Drawing and Discussion

Objectives:

The children will:
— identify respectful actions.
— describe an incident in which they demonstrated respect.
— creatively symbolize expressions of respect.

Materials:

art paper; scratch paper and pencils; colored marker or crayons; glue; decorative materials such as stickers, sequins, buttons, etc. (optional)

Directions:

Begin by asking the children to think of things that people do to show respect for one another. Focus on small courtesies like greeting a person, saying please and thank you, holding a door, letting someone go first, and shaking hands. Tell the children:

I've heard that some coaches insist that their players shake hands with the members of the opposing team after every game, regardless of whether they win or lose. Why would a coach do that? What message does the coach want to send the other team? What do the players learn by doing this?

After the children have had a few minutes to talk about this display of respect, announce that they are going to participate in an activity about respect, but in this activity instead of shaking hands, they'll draw hands.

Have the children work in pairs. Distribute the paper and pencils.

Instruct the children to take turns tracing each other's hand on a sheet of art paper. Point out that the drawing they end up with will be not of their own hand, but of their partner's hand. When they have finished tracing, explain the next step (in your own words):

Interview your partner to find out how your partner shows respect for other people. See if your partner can remember a specific time when he or she said or did something that demonstrated respect for a particular person. Take notes on your scratch paper. Then let your partner interview you. When both of you have finished, use what you've learned to illustrate the tracing of your partner's hand to show the respectful things your partner does. Use letters, symbols, pictures, and other decorations. Your illustration can symbolize lots of respectful actions, or it can tell the story of one particular incident. Decide who will be the first interviewer and get started.

Make available the art materials. List the following questions on the board to assist the children during their interviews:

Interview Questions:

- How do you show respect for other people?

- Can you remember a specific time when you did something for another person that showed respect? What happened?

When the children have finished their drawings, direct each pair to form a circle with two other pairs. Instruct the children to go around the circle and introduce their partner by showing their hand drawing and describing their partner's respectful actions.

Lead a culminating group discussion.

Discussion Questions:

1. A picture of two hands shaking is often used as a symbol of mutual respect and peace. Why do you think that is?
2. What are some other ways of showing respect that we included in our drawings?
3. If you offered to shake someone's hand and that person refused, what would you think?
4. Why is it important to show respect for others?
5. What would life be like if no one showed respect for anyone else.

A Web of Respect
Game, Discussion, and Poetry Reading

Objectives:

The children will:
— create a symbolic expression of their connectedness.
— describe positive qualities that they respect in one another.
— explain how the actions of one person in a group affect the actions of everyone else.

Materials:

a large ball of string; a copy of Chief Seattle's poem for each child (at end of activity) or the poem written on the board

Directions:

Have the children sit on the floor in a large circle. Determine which child's birthday is closest to the present date. Confer on that child both the ball of string and the honor of starting the activity. Instruct the child to grasp the end of the string and hold it while throwing the ball across the circle to another child.

Next, direct the child who threw the ball to say something positive about the child who catches it. In your own words, elaborate:

Look directly at the child who catches the ball of string, and describe one thing you respect and appreciate about that person. If you think he or she is friendly, humorous, athletic, helpful, loyal, musically talented, has nice hair, is a math whiz, or has a great smile — say that to the person. The "catcher" must accept the positive statement and can say "thank you" or "thanks," but nothing else. Holding onto the string, the catcher then throws the ball to another person in the circle and repeats the process. When it's your turn to throw the ball, you can aim at a specific person, but you must accept and speak to whomever catches the ball. With our throwing skills, we should be able to include everyone, with no repeats, the first time around.

Make sure the children continue to hold onto their portion of the string, keeping it fairly tight. When everyone has had at least one turn to throw and catch, and a web has been formed that connects everyone in the circle, tell the children that you would like to read them a poem written one and a half centuries ago by a Native American chief. Slowly read the poem at the end of this activity.

Give the children an opportunity to respond to the poem and its meaning. You may want to read it a second time. Then, direct the group to stand up carefully. Admire the web for a few final moments before asking the last person (the one holding the ball) to move around the group and rewind the string. If you have made handouts of the poem, distribute them. Otherwise, direct the attention of the children to the poem copied on the board. Refer to the poem while leading a final discussion.

Discussion Questions:

1. What does this poem say about respecting the earth and everything on the earth? Does that include people? Explain.
2. What is meant by the words, *All things are bound together. All things connect*?
3. In what ways are all of us in this group connected?
4. How are we connected to the rest of our afterschool? ...community? ...nation? ...earth?
5. What is meant by, *Whatever he does to the web, he does to himself*?
6. Can you describe an example showing how what one person in our group does affects everyone else?

All things are bound together.
All things connect.
What happens to the Earth
Happens to the children of the Earth.
Man has not woven the web of life.
He's but one thread.
Whatever he does to the web
He does to himself.
　　　—Chief Seattle, 1856

What I Like and Respect About Someone

A Sharing Circle

Objectives:

The children will:
— identify likable, respectable qualities in others.
— distinguish between feelings of liking and respect.
— describe something they can do to become more likable or worthy of respect.

Introduce the Topic:

Today our topic is, "What I Like and Respect About Someone." Each of us is going to think of a person for whom we feel admiration and respect, and try to pinpoint at least one quality in that person that causes us to have those feelings. Maybe the person works hard, or is very honest, or kind, or smart. Perhaps you like the person because he or she is friendly and accepts you the way you are, and perhaps you respect this person because he or she always keeps promises, treats people well, or gets involved in projects at school or in the community. Try to be specific. If you say that the person you like and respect is nice, try to describe one nice thing this person has done recently. Think it over for a few moments. The topic is, "What I Like and Respect About Someone."

Discussion Questions:

1. What kinds of things did we name that caused us to respect another person? ...to like another person?
2. What is the difference between liking a person and respecting the same person?
3. Can you like a person you don't respect? ...respect a person you don't like? Explain.
4. Which is more important to you, being liked or being respected? Why?
5. What have you learned from this session that will help you become a more likable person? ...a person others will respect?

How I Show Respect Toward Others

A Sharing Circle

Objectives:

The children will:
— identify specific behaviors that show respect.
— explain the difference between feeling respect and demonstrating it.
— state that how they act toward another person is a choice they make.

Introduce the Topic:

Our topic today is about showing respect, which is not the same as <u>having</u> respect. When you have respect for someone, you feel it inside; when you show respect, your actions demonstrate it. Our topic is, "How I Show Respect Toward Others."

Maybe you show your respect for people by being courteous and polite. Another way to show respect is to listen attentively when a person talks and not ridicule or make fun of what he says. Facial expressions can show respect or the lack of it; so can posture, gestures, and other types of body language. At times, showing respect can also mean leaving a person alone, not bothering her, allowing her to believe in, talk about, and do what she thinks is right for her. You might want to picture in your mind someone whom you respect and then think about how you act toward that person that shows your respect. Our topic is, "How I Show Respect Toward Others."

Discussion Questions:

1. What respectful actions were mentioned most during our circle?
2. How do you feel when someone shows respect for you?
3. Why is it important to demonstrate our respect for others?
4. What is the difference between having respect and showing it?
5. Who decides how you will act toward another person?

What Did You Learn About Respect?

Use this page to think about and record the things you have learned about respect. You can write, draw pictures, scribble and doodle, create a poem, or anything else that has meaning to you and will help you remember what you have learned.

When you finish, show this page to someone else and explain what you have learned.

Tips for Teaching Respect:

♥ When you speak with respect to your children, they learn respect. When you speak with disrespect, they learn that just as well. If you want them to do it, you must do it too

---

♥ When you see or hear your child using respectful language and making respectful choices, recognize it and praise him or her for it, and make sure to call your child on disrespectful behavior, too.

♥ Discuss the concept of respect with your child. Point out situations when you observe others being respected and disrespected. Ask your child how he or she would feel being the recipient of the respectful or disrespectful actions.

♥ Remind your child to be polite by saying things such as, "Please" and "Thank you." Explain that good manners are a way to show respect to others.

Dear Parents,

Your child will be embarking on a new program called Hearts and Minds at our afterschool site. We'll be learning important skills for getting along with others while developing valuable language abilities. Each time we begin a new unit, we'll send a letter home with your child which will tell you about the theme we're covering and how you can support it's development at home.

Currently, in our Hearts and Minds group, your child has been discovering what it means to respect someone and how to demonstrate respect. I encourage you to ask; "what did you learn today?"

We started out with a story, *How the Turkey Became a Star*. This is a story about Todd and Ralph. Ralph was a bully and always picked on Todd. It was a tough school year for Todd dealing with Ralph and he looked forward to the summer break. Todd went to summer camp where he discovered his talents and strengths. This helped Todd to feel like a star in his own right. When school started again, Todd felt good about himself. He was able to deal with Ralph in a confident manner. Though he avoided Ralph, he treated him with courtesy and insisted Ralph show some respect. Ralph ended up leaving Todd alone. As time went on, Ralph and Todd became friends.

With this story, other activities, and Sharing Circles we learned about ways to show respect, described respectable qualities in others, and distinguished between feelings of liking and respecting. Ask your child to share with you some of the things he or she learned about respect.

Happy learning together…

KINDNESS

— No act of kindness is ever wasted.

Aesop's Fables

— You can't assume that kindness is an inherited trait. It's learned behavior.

Katie Couric

Vocabulary Words

- Snickered
- Dreading
- Reluctantly
- Antennae
- Invade
- Tether ball

Four Eyes and Brace Face

by Beverly Ward Trust

"Boy, that sister of mine!" Scott grumbled, checking his watch again. "School's been out for fifteen minutes now and still no sign of her! She's becoming 'Miss Popularity' and I'm becoming 'Mr. Ex-Baseball Player.' If I'm late for one more practice, Coach Calen will..."

Out of the corner of his eye Scott saw Heather and her two friends running excitedly up the hill.

"Scott!" Heather called, panting for breath, "Quick! You gotta come with us!"

"Heather, I've got baseball practice!" Scott responded

"I know, Scott, this will only take a minute. You've gotta see this. Come on."

"Look, Scott!" Heather exclaimed. She pointed to a line of children waiting for a turn on the jungle gym.

"What am I supposed to be looking at?" He growled, feeling embarrassed at being in the middle of a group of giggling girls.

"Over there!" the three girls chanted. "Don't you see him?" — the boy in the blue shirt."

At that moment a little boy in a blue shirt turned around. He looked normal enough from the back, but when he turned around, Scott saw that the boy had braces. Not only braces, but the full head gear.

"So this is why I'm late for baseball practice?" Scott asked.

"Did you ever see anything so weird?" Janet snickered, "He looks like something from outer space!"

"Who is he?" Scott asked.

"He's the new boy in our class — or the new space creature I should say," Heather quipped.

"His name's Raymond," Sally said, "but everyone calls him BRACE FACE."

"Yeah, BRACE FACE FROM OUTER SPACE!" the girls shouted.

By this time the three girls were laughing so hard they were holding their sides. The little boy in the blue shirt could hear their laughter and knew they were laughing at him. Slowly, he turned his head, picked up his lunch box, and walked away.

"Well, that's great girls, I hope you're proud of yourselves!" Scott said.

"What do you mean, Scott?" Heather asked.

"Well, you were wrong! I've got better things to do than hurt somebody's feelings," Scott replied. "Like baseball practice!" And with that he turned and left.

"What's the matter with him?" Janet asked.

"I don't know, but I've got to go. See you tomorrow," Heather called as she ran to catch up with her brother.

The next morning, Heather, Sally, and Janet dashed to their desks just as their teacher was greeting the class.

"Good morning, boys and girls, who would like to do the attendance this morning?" Ms. Miller asked. Several hands went up. "Well, let's see, let's have someone new today. Would you like to, Raymond?"

"You mean BRACE FACE!" some voices blurted out from the back of the room. And with that, the whole class burst into laughter. Raymond was so embarrassed he threw his hands over his face and raced out of the room.

Ms. Miller turned to the class and demanded to know who had called out the name. "I can't believe that someone in this classroom has forgotten our most important rule," she said.

"Didn't we agree that we would treat others like we would like them to treat us? Well, someone here has treated Raymond very badly, and I'd like to know who that person is!"

Ms. Miller scanned every face. In the back of the room, three red-faced little girls were trying very hard to look normal. Both Janet and Sally nervously denied any guilt. "Heather, were you the one?" Ms. Miller asked. Heather could feel all the eyes in the classroom fixed right on her. The room was absolutely silent. She looked up at Ms. Miller painfully, as she considered the consequences of doing something wrong. Reluctantly, she whispered, "Yes, Ma'am, it was me."

"Well, Heather, I am certainly disappointed in your behavior. I'll see you after school today and we'll write down what happened in a letter to your parents."

Heather peeked up. "Yes, Ma'am," she whispered.

After school that day it was a long, nerve-wracking ride home. All the way home Heather worried about what her parents were going to do.

After dinner Scott asked, "When are you going to show the letter to them?" "Pretty soon, I guess," Heather said. "Well, good luck, Sis!" Scott said, going off to his room.

Heather slowly walked into the kitchen with the last dinner plate and her letter. "Are you feeling all right, tonight?" her mom asked.

Heather's stomach began to flip-flop. "Well, I ... uh ... I have a letter from Ms. Miller," she whispered.

Her mom smiled. "Another Top Citizen Award?" she asked.

Now, Heather felt worse than ever. "No," she sighed, "I think you'd better read it."

It seemed forever until her mother and father finished reading the letter and laid it down in the middle of the table. There was silence. This was the moment Heather had been dreading all day.

"Heather, you must know that your mother and I are very disappointed," her dad said. "We really didn't expect this from you."

"I have a question for you," her mom said, "and I want you to give me an honest answer."

"Okay," Heather said, nervously.

"Ms. Miller wrote that you were the one who called Raymond a name," she said, "but I have a feeling that Sally and Janet were in on this, too. Were they?"

Heather didn't want to lie. She didn't want to tell on her friends either, but her parents were staring at her and waiting for the truth. Reluctantly, she nodded her head.

Mother remarked, "A couple of times I've heard you girls laughing about the way other children look. Some people might call this innocent fun, but I think it's unkind and disrespectful."

"Perhaps you and Janet and Sally have a tendency to egg each other on," her dad said. "You get so wrapped up in your own games that you don't notice how cruel your put-downs are."

"I think you should spend the rest of the evening in your room thinking about a very important question," said Heather's mom.

"What question is that?" Heather asked.

"Think about what you and your friends did to Raymond in class today, and ask yourself, 'What if that were me?'"

Heather thought about this for a moment. "You mean what if that were me wearing braces and being teased?"

"That's right," Dad said, "and your mother and I expect a thoughtful answer from you in the morning before school. Right now it's late so you'd better go to your room and get started."

After Heather got into bed, she thought, "I guess I'd better start thinking if Mom and Dad expect an answer from me in the morning." She pulled the soft warm comforter up around her neck and snuggled down into the cool sheets. "WHAT IF THAT WERE ME?" she wondered, but before she could think of an answer, she fell fast asleep.

———————

"Good morning Ms. Miller," the children giggled.

"Well, you're all in a good mood today," Ms. Miller said, smiling. "What's so funny?"

"That's what's so funny!" Janet and Sally blurted out, pointing at Heather and laughing.

"Why, Heather, you do look different this morning," Ms. Miller remarked.

"Yeah," Janet snickered, "Like something from a different world!"

The whole class roared with laughter.

"I'll bet she's signaling her space ship right now with those antennae she's got on her head," Sally giggled.

Heather didn't have a clue about what was happening.

"Antennae? ... On my head?" She reached up to check her head and was suddenly shocked to find metal wires there. In a panic, she followed the wires down to her mouth and there she discovered a mouth of full metal. She had braces and head gear!

"Yeah," someone shouted, "any minute now her whole ship's likely to beam down and invade our classroom!"

"That's right! And they'll probably make all of us wear those things!" someone laughed.

"Oh, no!" the whole class chanted, "Then we'd all be BRACE FACES!"

Heather was so embarrassed! She prayed the floor would open up and swallow her. How could her friends and classmates be so cruel?

"How could they?" she moaned, tossing and turning. Then, suddenly, she awoke with a jolt. Her heart was pounding wildly.

———————

Heather's fingers flew to her mouth. "Oh!" she sighed with relief. "What a terrible nightmare!" Heather was so upset that she scrambled out of bed and rushed down the hall to her parents' bedroom.

"You're okay, honey," her mom whispered. "Everything's all right now."

"Tell us about it?" her dad suggested, patting her back.

Heather explained every detail of the nightmare — especially how badly her friends and classmates had treated her and how terrible the put-downs made her feel.

Dad took Heather's hand and said gently, "We can imagine the hurt you felt in your dream when all your friends were calling you names. It must have been terrible. But, you know, this nightmare just might have taught you something."

Heather was silent for a few minutes as she thought. "Now I know how badly Raymond must feel when people put him down because he has braces. It must seem like a nightmare to him every day. I don't understand why his parents make him wear those things."

"Well," her mom said, "what if you woke up one morning, looked in the mirror and discovered a mouthful of crooked, twisted teeth? You couldn't speak clearly or chew food properly, and your friends called you Snaggletooth."

"Oh, no!" Heather groaned, "this sounds like another nightmare."

"But what would you do if it were true?" Dad asked.

"I'd want you to fix my teeth — quick!"

"But that would mean braces for a couple years," Dad explained.

"I know," Heather sighed, "but I think I'd rather be called Brace Face for a couple years than Snaggletooth for the rest of my life!"

"That must be what Raymond's parents thought too," her mom explained.

"They want to make life better for him in the future. I'll bet there's something you could do to make Raymond's life better, too."

"Like apologize?" Heather asked.

"That's a good start," her mom said. "And, who knows, maybe you'll make a new friend."

The next day at school the first thing Heather did was apologize to Raymond. She told him she'd like to be his friend and she invited him to play a game of tether ball before the bell rang. It was a lot of fun!

She didn't talk with Janet or Sally until lunch time when they came running up to ask her what it was like sitting next to FOUR EYES.

"Four Eyes?" Heather asked.

"Yeah, Laura with her new glasses — FOUR EYES!" they snickered.

"It's just as nice sitting next to Laura as it always was — she's a good friend," Heather said. "She's coming to our slumber party Saturday. You'll like her. It'll be nice having someone new join us. I can't wait 'till the party. And, boy," Heather giggled, "do I have a dream to tell you two!

Discussion Questions:

1. Why were Heather and her friends unkind to Raymond?
2. How do you think Raymond felt when Heather and her friends were putting him down? Why didn't the girls consider his feelings?
3. How did Heather feel in her dream? How did the dream change her attitude toward Raymond?
5. What is a put-down? What are some examples of put-downs?
6. Is there any such thing as a "kind" put-down? Explain.
7. What does it mean to be kind?
8. What is the "Golden Rule?"
9. How can we use the Golden Rule to guide our actions toward other people?
10. What are some specific ways that we can show each other kindness here at our afterschool site?

Four Eyes and Brace Face

Experience Sheet

Think about the story, "Four Eyes and Brace Face." What thoughts do you have about the characters? How did you react to the things they said and did? Use this page to write down your thoughts as you answer the questions.

1. Have you ever been the object of teasing or put-downs? How did you feel and what did you do?

2. Think of someone you know who is very kind. What are some of the kind things this person does?

3. Describe an act of kindness that you have done for someone recently:

4. Think of six kind acts that you can do for friends or family members during the next week. List them here:

A Book of Kindness
Writing and Art Activity

Objectives:

The children will:
— define the term kindness.
— brainstorm examples of kind deeds.
— describe a kind act they did or received.

Materials:

writing materials; drawing paper; colored marking pens, crayons, or pencils; glue; a large three-ring binder

Directions:

Write the word kindness on the board. Ask the children to help you define its meaning. In the process, make these points about kindness:

- Kindness is a quality that is developed from being kind.
- Being kind means being considerate, thoughtful, or helpful.
- An act of kindness is something you do. It is a deed or behavior. It's possible to have kind thoughts and feelings, but they are private until you express them in an act of kindness.
- A kind act is always done voluntarily, not because it is required.

Ask the children to brainstorm examples of kind acts. List their suggestions on the board. Encourage a variety of ideas, by asking questions like "What are some kind acts you can do for a friend? ...a classmate? ...brother or sister?

...parent? ...neighbor? ...your teacher? ...grandparent? ...a stranger? ...the environment? Include things like:

— make friends with a new child
— offer to share things
— talk to or play with kids who seem left out
— give someone a compliment
— read a story to a younger child
— visit senior citizens in a retirement or rest home
— help a friend do his or her chores
— help a classmate solve a tough math problem
— surprise your parent by doing an "extra" chore at home
— hold a door for someone
— pick up trash when you see it lying around

Announce that the children are going to write about and draw an act of kindness they've done — or one that someone else has done for them. Distribute writing and drawing materials. In your own words, explain:

Describe the kind act, tell who did it, and for whom it was done. You don't have to mention names, just use words like "friend," "teacher," "sister," or "older person." Then write about the feelings of the person who did the kind deed, and the feelings of the person who received it. Draw a picture that shows the kind act being done.

Use whatever system you normally use to have the children correct their spelling and grammar and then complete a rewrite. As a final step, have the children assemble the story and drawing, either by writing a final version somewhere on the drawing itself, or by gluing the drawing to the story page, or vice-versa.

Have the children share their stories and pictures in small groups. Then place all of the finished work in the three-ring binder. Insert a cover page titled, "Book of Kindness."

Discussion Questions:

1. Why is it important to try to turn kind thoughts into kind deeds?
2. When you have a kind thought about someone, how can you express it?
3. Why can't chores and assignments ever be acts of kindness?
4. Why do acts of kindness have to be voluntary?

Kindness Coupons
A Writing and Design Project

Objectives:

The children will:
— identify kind acts that can be done for different people.
— commit to future acts of kindness by describing them in writing.

Materials:

samples of coupons or coupon books; 8 1/2-inch by 11-inch sheets of sturdy white paper cut horizontally into three equal pieces (8 1/2 by 3 2/3); several sheets of colored construction paper cut to the same size or slightly larger; colored markers, pencils or crayons; decorative stickers (optional); stapler

Directions:

On the board, write the headings **Parents, Friend, Brother/Sister, Grandparents**. Ask the children to help you list acts of kindness that they could do for each of these people. For example:

Parents
wash dishes
give a massage
give a big hug
watch the baby
give a compliment
carry the groceries
clean and sort a drawer or shelf

When you have generated several items under each heading, announce that the children are each going to make a Kindness Coupon Book to give to their parents or to some other person. Each page will have a coupon that can be torn out and redeemed for a specific act of kindness. A description of the kind action will be written on the page. The children can decorate the coupons with borders, fancy lettering, symbols, drawings, or stickers (if available).

Give each child six to ten sheets of cut white paper and two pieces of cut colored construction paper. Have the children make a sharp crease in each white sheet about 1–1/2 inches from the left edge. Tell them not to draw or write on the left section because this is where the coupons will be stapled together. The crease will allow for easy tearing.

Make two coupons yourself to demonstrate the process. On each coupon write or print a description of a kind action and any instructions for receiving it. For example, "5-Minute Back Massage — Good any evening 6:00 - 8:00 p.m." Decorate with a drawing of a hand or some other symbol. Make a second sample. Then place the coupons between two pieces of colored construction paper to create front and back covers. Staple the left edge securely. On the front cover, print "Kindness Coupon Book" in large dark letters.

Make the art materials available to the children. Circulate to make sure that children who do not want to make a book for parents have chosen another recipient, e.g., a grandparent or friend. Encourage the children to collaborate.

Allow time for the children to circulate and informally share their finished books.

Discussion Questions:

1. Why do acts of kindness — even very small ones — make the recipient happy?
2. Do you sometimes need permission before doing something for a person? When?
3. What could you say or do if your parent turned in a coupon when you didn't feel like doing the kind act?

Variation:

You may prefer to have the children make a coupon book to carry with them, rather than give to someone else. The coupons are torn out by the child and given to different people, then redeemed by those people for specific acts of kindness. This method allows the child to control the process, which ensures that the kind acts are always voluntary. Be sure to provide opportunity for the children to share when they have given out a coupon and to tell what happened.

A Time I Felt Sorry for Someone Who Was Put Down

A Sharing Circle

Objectives:

The children will:
— express empathy for the feelings of another person.
— describe some of the negative effects of put-downs.
— explain why people use put-downs.
— describe ways of avoiding the habit of putting others down.

Introduce the topic:

Today, we're going to talk about put-downs and how they affect people. Our topic is, "A Time I Felt Sorry for Someone Who Was Put Down." Unfortunately, people seem to put each other down a lot these days. In addition, we see put-downs all the time on television. Many of those put-downs are supposed to come across as clever. This is unfortunate, because put-downs hurt people — even those that are intended as jokes.

Try to remember a time when you observed someone say or do something that made another person feel bad. Maybe the put-down was done as a joke or perhaps it was intended to be hurtful. The incident may have occurred at school, in the neighborhood, at the supermarket or shopping mall, or somewhere else. Without mentioning any names, tell us what happened, how you reacted, and how you think the person who was put down felt. Think it over for a few moments. The topic is, "A Time I Felt Sorry for Someone Who Was Put Down."

Discussion Questions:

1. How did most of us react to seeing another person put down?
2. How do you feel when someone puts you down?
3. Why do people put each other down?
4. How can you prevent yourself from getting in the "put-down" habit?

Something I Did to Make Someone Feel Good

A Sharing Circle

Objectives:

The children will:
— identify specific words and actions that create good feelings in others.
— accept credit for good and kind deeds.
— explain how acts of kindness benefit themselves and others.

Introduce the Topic:

Today's topic is a very broad one that can be discussed in many ways. It is, "Something I Did to Make Someone Feel Good." You see what I mean? You have probably done hundreds of things to make other people feel good. Just tell us about one.

Maybe you gave someone a flower, a present, or a compliment. Perhaps you hugged a friend who was feeling bad, or offered to relieve a parent of a chore or errand. Telling a joke can make someone feel good. So can telling a person what a good job he or she did, or saying, "I like you" or "I love you." Describe what you said or did and how you felt inside. The topic is, "Something I Did to Make Someone Feel Good."

Discussion Questions:

1. How do you feel when you know you've made someone feel good?
2. Usually, when a person feels good, everyone who comes in contact with that person benefits. Can you explain how that happens?
3. If everyone in our group tried to make one extra person feel good each day, how would our group benefit?

What Did You Learn About Kindness?

Use this page to think about and record the things you have learned about kindness. You can write, draw pictures, scribble and doodle, create a poem, or anything else that has meaning to you and will help you remember what you have learned.

When you finish, show this page to someone else and explain what you have learned.

Tips for Teaching Kindness:

♡ If your child sees someone being treated unkindly (or your child is being unkind to someone), ask what it would be like to be in the other person's shoes. Ask how it would feel if someone treated him or her that way?

♡ If you give or receive a special acknowledgment or "thank you", share your feelings and gratitude with your child. The importance of kindness will sink in when your child sees how important kind words are to you.

♡ Model thoughtful and kind behaviors. Everything you say and do teaches your child something. Be mindful of what you are teaching. Be kind, thoughtful, and polite. Sincerely compliment others. Etc.

♡ Talk with your child about people you think are kind to others. Together, describe those behaviors, and discuss ways he or she can act in those kind ways too.

Dear Parents,

Today in our Hearts and Minds group, we discovered what it means to show kindness and how to be kind.

We started out with a story, *Four Eyes and Brace-Face*. This is a story about Heather who gets in trouble for teasing another child in her class because of the way he looked. Heather learns through a terrible dream, how another person could really feel when they are put down and teased.

When we discussed this story, the children identified ways to show kindness, described acts of kindness they did or received, and identified kind acts that can be done for different people. In our Sharing Circle we discussed ways to express empathy toward the feelings of others while identifying words and actions that would create good feelings in others. The children had awesome thoughts and comments. Ask your child what we talked about. I'm sure you will be happy with what you hear.

Happy talking and sharing together…

TOLERANCE

— Peace is not won by those who fiercely guard their differences, but by those who with open minds and hearts seek out connections.

Katherine Patterson

— Just imagine how boring life would be if we were all the same. My idea of a perfect world is one in which we really appreciate each others differences.

Barbra Striesand

Vocabulary Words

- Imbedded
- Guff
- Intently
- Gesturing
- Rummaging
- Research

Randy Learns About Tolerance
by Dianne Schilling

Tolerance. The word was everywhere. In big plastic letters on the sign outside the main office, just below where it said Kennedy Elementary School. Lettered across the top of bulletin boards in all the classrooms. Imbedded in colorful posters hung throughout the halls. On the inside curved walls of the school buses. Tolerance — the word of the month.

Well, it was more than a word. Tolerance was the *moral value* of the month. Last month the moral value was Kndness and the month before it was Respect. In January, the first month to have a value, all the signs said Honesty.

On Monday, Ms. Bartels told her 5th-grade class to look up the meaning of the word. "After you've done your research, be thinking about what tolerance means to you," she said. "Next week, I'll ask you to share some of your ideas."

"It's hard *not* to think about it," eleven-year-old Randy sighed to himself. "Tolerance is everywhere you look."

That evening, as Randy and his dad, Henry, were clearing away the dinner dishes, Henry looked at his wife and asked, "Why are you so tired tonight, Corinne?"

"Phil was out sick again today. The office was super busy and I had to do his work plus my own," answered Randy's mom, wearily scooping spilled applesauce from the front of Jesse's coveralls. Jesse was Randy's baby brother.

"You're too *tolerant*, Corinne. Phil misses work all the time. He takes advantage of you. If you weren't so willing to cover for him, he'd have been fired long ago," Randy's dad said.

"But what if he really is sick, Henry? The least I can do is help."

"What does *tolerant* mean?" Randy interrupted.

"What?" Randy's mother looked startled, like she'd forgotten Randy was there.

"Dad said you're too tolerant," Randy repeated. "What's 'tolerant'?"

"It means your mother puts up with too much guff from Phil," said Henry firmly. "She should put her foot down."

"Now Henry, I know you're thinking of me, but you don't understand what it's like at my office," Corrine argued.

Randy was puzzled by his father's reply, but he decided not to interrupt again.

"You're feeding the baby table foods Corinne? Isn't it too soon?" asked Aunt Rita, who stopped by every Tuesday with ideas and advice for everyone.

"Jess seems to *tolerate* them just fine, Aunt Rita. Don't worry, I'm not giving him meat or olives or anything. Just soft things." Intently, Jesse worked several slippery strands of spaghetti into his mouth.

"Mom, he really *likes* the spaghetti," said Randy.

"Yes, Randy. That's what I was telling Aunt Rita."

"No...., you said Jess *tolerates* it. That means he puts up with it. But I think he likes it," insisted Randy.

"I meant his *system* tolerates solid food, Randy. You know — his stomach. Sometimes babies can't eat what everybody else eats. But Jesse's system tolerates it." explained Corrine.

"What would happen if his system didn't tolerate it, Mom?" asked Randy.

"He'd spit it up," Aunt Rita declared. "So be careful — tolerance has its limits!"

Randy made a face. That was a strange kind of tolerance.

"Have you seen the new boy who moved in on the corner?" Randy asked his mother. "He looks funny."

"Yes, I've seen him from a distance," answered Corrine. "He has come from Africa to live with the Stewarts. He may look a little different from most of the folks we know, Randy. Maybe he even does some things a little differently. But inside I'm sure he's a lot like you."

"He'll probably go to my school. He's in for trouble if he does," Randy thought out loud.

"What do you mean?" demanded Corrine. "Why would there be trouble?"

"Because he's different, Mom. If you don't fit in, you get teased. Kids say things."

Randy's mother snorted angrily and slammed her open palm on the kitchen counter. "Something is seriously wrong if we can't have a little *tolerance* for each other's differences," she said. "I expect you to be nice to that new boy, Randy."

"Do you mean I should put up with him?" asked Randy, "Or do you mean he shouldn't make my stomach sick?" Randy was experimenting with the word *tolerance*, but his mother didn't think it was funny.

"Tolerance means accepting other people," said Corrine sternly. "Everybody can't be just like us."

Sure enough, the new boy from the Stewart house was at school the very next day. And he was in Randy's class.

"Children, this is Josephat Nmbura. Josephat is from Tanzania, which is a country in Africa," said Ms. Bartels, gesturing toward the thin, dark boy seated near the front of the room.

The new boy jumped to his feet and smiled broadly, revealing a gap in his lower front teeth. "I am being happy to know American school," he said, his words thickly accented. Several children laughed.

"Josephat is learning English," smiled Ms. Bartels, "so be sure to help him. Ernesto, would you like to find Tanzania on the map and show the rest of us where it is?"

While Ernesto studied the big world map on the wall, two dozen pairs of eyes studied Josephat. Randy tried to figure out what was different about him. At least half the class was African-American, so it wasn't his skin color. Maybe it was the way he sat so straight, and the way he kept smiling. His clothing was like the other boys, but his hair was shaved close to his head. Then Randy saw the circles. A small round mark, like the imprint from a bottle cap, high on each cheek. Randy wondered why a kid would paint circles on his face.

During recess, Randy and two friends checked out a soccer ball and practiced kicks and fancy footwork on the grass. Their breathless attempts to outdo each other were interrupted by loud laughter coming from the lunch tables a few yards away. Curious, they stopped their game and moved in that direction.

Several children were gathered around Josephat. Some were laughing and pointing. Others were huddled together whispering and giggling. Josephat, smiling as always, looked confused. The empty space between his teeth made him look a little dumb, too, Randy thought.

Gary, a big sixth-grader who was always acting smart, said to the group, "He gave me most of his lunch! Half the sandwich, the apple, most of the cookies. Every time he pulled something out of the bag, he handed it to me. Then he acted like I was supposed to give him *my* lunch. I guess he thought we were having a picnic!" Gary doubled over laughing.

Randy thought about tolerance. He remembered little Jess and Aunt Rita, and wondered if it was his turn to be sick. Instead, he took a deep breath and yelled to Gary and anyone else who was listening, "Leave Josephat alone. So what if he thought it was a picnic? Maybe they have picnics in Africa."

Seconds later, the bell rang. The children quickly forgot about Josephat and headed for their classrooms. Randy walked silently beside

Josephat. Out of the corner of his eye, he studied the circle on Josephat's left cheek. It wasn't painted on; it was part of Josephat's skin. "A scar," Randy thought.

All afternoon, and for the next two days, Josephat kept the kids in Randy's class amused. Every time Ms. Bartels called on him or even mentioned his name, Josephat jumped to his feet, grinning. Twice Randy laughed with the other kids and then felt guilty. The first time Ms. Bartels asked Josephat to help pass out some papers, he answered very seriously, "Yes, Mama." All the kids looked at each other in disbelief, then burst out laughing. For the rest of the day, Ms. Bartels was "Mama" to some of the class clowns. "Yes Mama" this, and "Yes Mama" that.

Josephat's English was slow and oddly phrased. Randy could see smirks and hear giggles every time Josephat spoke. Two boys in the back of the room made a game of imitating Josephat's stiff posture.

All the while *Tolerance* in big black bulletin-board letters loomed over the class. Like the giant oak tree in front of the school, *Tolerance* was part of the scenery — so nobody saw it.

On Saturday morning, Bob came over from next door to help Henry with the room addition. The breakfast nook was becoming a family room and part of the back yard was being lost in the process.

"What's the *tolerance* of that window opening, Henry?" Bob asked.

"Oh, about a half-inch, I think."

"*Tolerance*, Dad? Are you sure Bob meant *tolerance*?" asked Randy.

"Sure, son. Tolerance is how much leeway we have in choosing a window to fit the opening. The measurements have to be close, but they don't have to be exact. We can tighten up the fit when we add the frame around the window."

Randy picked up a measuring tape from the floor and checked the size of the window opening. He pushed the button on the metal case and watched the tape shoot back inside. He was surprised that tolerance could be measured.

Randy wandered into the living room, used his foot to push Jess's abandoned toys out of the way, and sprawled on the nubby beige carpet.

He decided to watch a video. Rummaging through stacks of DVDs, Randy found one of his favorites and, in seconds, tolerance was far from his mind — but not for long. Twenty minutes into *Raiders of the Lost Ark*, Randy's mother huffed through the doorway and shouted above the noise, "Randy, I will not tolerate the condition of your room a moment longer! Get in there and do something about it, and no more TV until it's clean!"

Randy groaned and flicked off the DVD. "Will tolerate, won't tolerate, too tolerant, not tolerant enough," he thought. "I think *everybody's* confused about tolerance."

On Sunday afternoon, Duane and Michael came over. They played computer games and rode their bikes to the park where they sat on the grass and talked about summer vacation.

"If you could do anything you wanted this summer, what would you choose?" asked Randy.

Duane thought a minute. "I'd go on one of those cruises," he said. "My cousin went on a Caribbean cruise and ended up with three days at Disney World. That'd be cool."

"What about you, Michael?" asked Randy.

"I'd go visit my grandfather in Idaho and go fishing," answered Michael. "Gramps knows all the best rivers and camping spots."

"If I could do anything," said Randy, "I'd work at the zoo this summer. Sometimes they let kids have jobs as keeper's aides."

"That's a stupid idea," said Duane. "If you could do anything you wanted, why stay here? You're here all year long. Go to Hawaii or Paris or China."

"It's not a stupid idea," said Randy. "I want to learn about animals."

"But that's like school," said Michael. "You probably get graded and everything. Duane's right. Do something fun, not something nerdy."

"Randy's always a nerd," said Duane. "He doesn't know what fun is."

"Oh yeah, why'd you come over today then?" asked Randy. "If I'm so boring, why come to my house at all?"

"Because I couldn't think of anything better to do, that's why," said Duane. "Com'on Mike, let's go. I don't want to keep 'Randa-the-Panda' from dreaming about the zoo."

As Randy rode his bike home, he thought about what his friends had said. He really did want to work at the zoo. He had a right to his own idea of fun. Duane and Michael were just being selfish. They were being…

"Intolerant," Randy said out loud. The word popped out from some corner of his brain, surprising him and causing him to swerve sharply. He had just rounded the corner in front of the Stewart's house, and a friendly voice called out, "Hey, slow down Randy! It's not even dinner time!"

It was Mr. Stewart working inside his open garage. Randy was embarrassed. He must have been riding faster than he realized. He pulled his bike around and stopped. Getting off, he let the bike drop gently on the front lawn. "Sorry, Mr. Stewart," Randy said, walking into the garage.

"You must have been thinking hard about something," laughed Mr. Stewart. "You've met Josephat, haven't you?"

It was then that Randy saw Josephat, sitting on a stool near the back of the garage. Josephat smiled and stood up. Randy said hello. He couldn't think of anything else to say, and the two boys just stood there looking at each other self-consciously.

After a moment, Mr. Stewart looked around from his workbench. "Josephat, why don't you take Randy inside and get him a glass of water."

"Oh, no thanks," said Randy quickly. "I'd better be getting home."

"What's the hurry?" asked Mr. Stewart. "Like I said, it's not even dinner time. And besides, Josephat needs the practice." Mr. Stewart winked at Randy, making it impossible for him to leave.

Josephat poured two glasses of water and gave one to Randy, who drank it thirstily. "Thanks," Randy said, setting the empty glass on the counter. He looked at Josephat and felt stupidly speechless. Finally, he asked, "Want to show me your room?"

"My room?" repeated Josephat. "Oh, yes. Come."

Josephat's small room had what looked to Randy like African pictures on the walls, along with framed photographs of people in large and small groups. Josephat explained that these were school friends in Tanzania. Carved animals sat in groups on the dresser, bookcase, and bedside table. "Wow," said Randy, picking up a painted wood giraffe.

"You like the giraffe? Please, you must have it," said Josephat.

"No, no," Randy said politely. "It's yours. Randy's finger traced the smooth surface of a carved elephant.

"Then take elephant," insisted Josephat.

Every time Randy saw something he liked, Josephat tried to give it to him. Randy stopped admiring Josephat's things, and instead looked at Josephat. His eyes went to the circles on Josephat's cheeks.

"All boys have," explained Josephat. "In Maasai tribe, a sign of beauty," he said. He pointed to his cheeks and said, "Only boys." Then he pointed to the gap where his lower front tooth had been cut out, saying, "Girls, too." Josephat laughed and said, "I must get a tooth for America. Not beautiful here."

Josephat and Randy both laughed.

On Monday morning, Ms. Bartels pointed to the word *Tolerance* on the bulletin board. She asked the children to reflect on what they learned about tolerance during the past week. She told them to write at least five sentences about tolerance, and then she asked volunteers to read what they had written. Randy raised his hand. When Ms. Bartels called on him, he read:

Tolerance is putting up with something you don't like.

Tolerance is being able to eat something without getting sick.

Tolerance is when a window or door doesn't have to fit exactly.

Tolerance is when it's okay for your friend to spend his summer doing something that he thinks is fun — even if you don't think it's fun.

Tolerance is accepting when a person looks different or has different ideas or different ways of doing things.

When the noon bell rang, Randy took his lunch and went outside. He found Josephat sitting at a lunch table and scooted in next to him. Randy opened his lunch. He took out a sandwich, grapes, carrot sticks, and cookies. He spread everything out on the table. Josephat did the same. Then Randy gave half of everything he had to Josephat who, laughing, did the same in return.

When other kids walked by, Randy said, "Josephat and I are having a picnic. Want to join us? Several children did.

Discussion Questions:

1. What were the different definitions of tolerance that Randy discovered?
2. Why did the other children make fun of Josephat?
3. How was Josephat different from the other children? How was he the same?
4. How do you think Josephat felt as a new child in a strange country?
5. What does it mean to recognize the beliefs and practices of another person?
6. Does recognizing and accepting a person's beliefs and practices mean that you have to agree with them or make them your own? Explain.

Randy Learns About Tolerance

Experience Sheet

Randy's teacher told the children to think about what tolerance meant to them. Here's a place to write about what tolerance means to you:

2. Has anyone ever been intolerant of you or something about you? What happened and how did you feel?

1. Why do you think it is important to be tolerant of people who have different beliefs and customs than you have?

3. When have you demonstrated tolerance for someone or something?

To tolerate means to Put up with???

? Tolerance ?
T = 1 to 2 inches

Recognize and Accept

Meet Pebble Pete

An Experiment in the Recognition of Unique Characteristics

Objectives:

The children will:
— describe the unique characteristics of one member of a group of similar objects.
— compare the stereotyping of objects to the stereotyping of people.
— explain that it is the responsibility of the viewer to differentiate one person from another.

Materials:

a paper bag containing a collection of small rocks or pebbles, all very similar in size, shape, and color (apples, oranges, potatoes, or nuts may be substituted)

Directions:

Begin by asking the children: *Have you ever noticed how people tend to generalize about other people? By "generalize," I mean lump people together in groups. We usually only do that with people we don't know very well. It's hard to stereotype a friend.*

Have the children sit in a large circle. Open the paper bag and show the pebbles to the children. In your own words, say:

These pebbles all look pretty much the same at first glance. But that's because you don't know them. Therefore, I'm going to give you an opportunity to meet and become acquainted with one of these pebbles.

Pass around the bag full of pebbles and have each child reach in and take one. When the bag returns to you, choose a pebble for yourself. Direct the children to take 1 minute to examine their pebble very carefully — to notice its features and everything unique about it so they can introduce it to the group. After 1 minute, begin the sharing by introducing your own pebble. For example, say something like:

I'd like you to meet Pebble Pete. Pete began his life on a mountainside in New Mexico. When he was first chipped from his mother, who was a big boulder, he hit the ground and kept sliding — right down the mountain! That experience scratched him up quite a bit. During his first winter, he was washed into a river and spent almost four years traveling downstream. The water smoothed him out, but I can still see one or two scratches on this side. Finally Pete came ashore near the wide mouth of the river and was eventually scooped up by a man who collected pebbles in his pickup truck and sold them to the landscapers and nurseries in town. That's how I met Pebble Pete. Now he has a job on a pathway in my garden.

Go around the circle and invite the children to introduce their pebbles to the group. When the last pebble has been introduced, thank the children. Then pass the empty bag around, instructing the children to return their pebble to the collection. (Be sure you remove any extra pebbles from the bag before you recollect.)

Ask the children: *Now that you and your pebble have become friends, do you think that it will still look just like all the other pebbles? Let's find out. I'm going to put all the pebbles in the center of the circle so that you can find yours and take it back. The last pebble on the floor should be Pebble Pete.*

Roll the pebbles out of the bag onto the floor. Allow two or three children at a time to examine the pebbles, identify the one they had, and take their pebble "friend" back to their seat. (If someone takes Pete by mistake, express your concern and check the children's pebbles to find him and trade.) Conclude the activity with a discussion.

Discussion Questions:

1. Have you ever heard someone say, "They're all alike"? What will you think the next time you hear that expression?
2. Why do people lump others into groups and pretend they are all alike?
3. What can you say or do if you hear someone stereotyping a person based on color, sex, religion, or some other characteristic?
4. Whose job is it to see and acknowledge the differences between one person and another?

Extension:

Allow the children to decorate their pebbles with miniature designs. Have them apply opaque paints with the tips of small brushes or with Q-tips.

If the Shoe Fits

An Experiment in Categorizing

Objectives:

The children will:
— categorize objects according to a variety of criteria.
— explain that a category both includes and excludes members.
— list categories into which we routinely group people.
— discuss the benefits and drawbacks of categorizing people.

Materials:

a variety of single shoes — old, new, dress, casual, sandals, sneakers, child's, adult's, representing a variety of colors, sizes, styles and heel heights (the more samples, the better); instead of real shoes, you could provide pictures of shoes from catalogs and advertisements

Directions:

Have the children sit in a circle. Spread the shoes out on the floor in the center of the circle.

Ask the children to look at the shoes and come up with suitable categories for grouping the shoes. (In addition to the categories mentioned under "Materials," you might have shoes that are athletic, hiking, formal, orthopedic, rain, snow, etc.)

Next, see if you can pair the categories. For example:

child	adult
dress	casual
old	new
leather	fabric

  high heel   low heel
  open   closed

 Taking one set of categories at a time, have the children physically arrange the shoes into the two groups. Ask the children to notice:
— Which shoes don't seem to fit either category and are therefore "left out" after each grouping.
— Which shoes fit the most categories and which the fewest.
— Which categories are more inclusive and which are less.
— Which categories seem better than others and why.
— How they decide where to put a shoe when it fits two categories equally.
— If they try to bend or stretch a category so that a shoe fits.

 Talk about the purpose of having categories and groups. Who is helped by grouping and labeling shoes? Point out that whenever a category is created to include certain items, it automatically excludes others. In a culminating discussion, turn the attention of children from shoes to people, and examine how these concepts and insights apply to the categorizing of people, too. Brainstorm and list all the different people categories that the children can think of. Refer to the list throughout the discussion.

Discussion Questions:

1. How do we categorize people?
2. Who is helped by categorizing people?
3. What groups of people have not been accepted by the dominant culture during our history? How were they treated?
4. How do you feel when you are excluded (left out)?
5. How do groups of people feel when the culture excludes or limits them? What do they do?

A Friend I Have Who Is Different From Me

A Sharing Circle

Objectives:

The children will:
— demonstrate that friendships form across racial, cultural, and other types of boundaries.
— describe the relative importance of commonalties and differences in a friendship.

Introduce the Topic:

Today we're going to talk about our friends, particularly the ones who are different from us in some significant way. Our topic is, "A Friend I Have Who Is Different From Me."

Tell us about a friend of yours who is either much older or much younger, is of a different race or culture, or is very different from you in some other way. Tell us how you became friends with this person and what you like about him or her. I'll give you a few moments to decide what you want to share. Our topic is, "A Friend I Have Who Is Different From Me."

Discussion Questions:

1. What were the reasons we gave for liking these friends and valuing their friendship?
2. What, if any, problems or conflicts have been caused by the difference between you and your friend, and how have you handled them?
3. What have you and your friend been able to learn from each other as a result of your differences?
4. What is more important between friends, the things you have in common or your differences? Why?

A Way I Show Tolerance

A Sharing Circle

Objectives:

The children will:
— describe examples of tolerant behavior.
— recognize that a multicultural society includes people of different beliefs who have different ways of doing things.

Introduce the Topic:

Tolerance is a very important word in our language. It also conveys a very important idea. Tolerance means recognizing and accepting the beliefs and practices of others, especially when they are different from our own. Today, we're going to talk about what it means to recognize and accept another person's beliefs and ways of doing things. Our topic is, "A Way I Show Tolerance."

How do you show your friends, classmates and family member that it's okay with you if they have different beliefs than you have, and do things in different ways? When someone says something you don't agree with, do you listen carefully and see what you can learn? Maybe you say something like, "That's your opinion, but I have a different one," or "That's interesting," or "Let me see if I understand you." Or perhaps you just remain quiet and don't say anything. Think about this carefully. Out topic is, "A Way I Show Tolerance."

Discussion Questions:

1. Can you think of anything you do every day that couldn't be done in a different way?
2. Why do people get into arguments and fights over the "right" answer or the "right" way of doing something?
3. Why is it important to show tolerance for the beliefs and practices of others?

What Did You Learn About Tolerance?

Use this page to think about and record the things you have learned about tolerance. You can write, draw pictures, scribble and doodle, create a poem, or anything else that has meaning to you and will help you remember what you have learned.

When you finish, show this page to someone else and explain what you have learned.

Tips for Teaching Tolerance:

♥ Talk about differences respectfully. Talk about the differences among your family and friends (hair color, skin color, personal likes and dislikes), and use the opportunity to talk about how it's good that people are different. You could also discuss how people are the same as well (i.e. you have blonde hair and your friend has brown hair, but you are both girls and you both have two eyes, two ears, one mouth, etc.).

♥ Promote openness and respect by demonstrating empathy and compassion through your words and actions. Besides not letting your child bully or tease someone else, watch what you say yourself! Treat others with respect, and your child will, too. Even comments about your own body can lead a child to make judgments about other people.

♥ Encourage self-confidence. A child who is confident about him or herself will be more likely to embrace differences and see the value in others.

Dear Parents,

Today in our Hearts and Minds group, your child discovered a very important word, *tolerance*. Tolerance conveys the idea of recognizing and accepting the beliefs and practices of others, especially when they are different from our own. I encourage you to ask your child what was learned today. If you hear, "nothing", like kids often say, let me give you a heads up as to what we did.

We started out with a story, "Randy Learns About Tolerance." This is a story about Randy discovering the meaning of tolerance. Randy had one week to research the new word and come up with what tolerance means to him. Randy kept his ears open at home and heard several scenarios that called out the new vocabulary word. From his mother being tolerant at work and his baby brother tolerating table food, to stereotyping, categorizing and defining unique characteristics of other. Your child will also be doing a group experiment with the recognition of unique characteristics. Ask about the pebble towards the end of the week!

In our Sharing Circle we talked about personal experiences with tolerance. Ask your child what was learned from the discussion. You will be happy with what you may hear.

Happy sharing thoughts together…

SERVICE TO OTHERS

— An essential part of a happy, healthy life is being of service to others.
Sue Patton Thoele

— Service to others is the rent you pay for your room here on earth.
Mohammed Ali

Vocabulary Words

- Blurted
- Haste
- Materializing
- Invention
- Service
- Volunteers

Marvin's Last Invention

by Tom Pettepiece

Marvin was always inventing something strange.

Once he invented a bubble gum that lasted four days without losing its flavor. Another time he invented a machine that let you eat dinner, listen to your parents and do your homework all at once so you'd have more time to play.

Half of what he invented never worked, and most of the kids thought he was crazy. But this, he thought, was his best invention yet — the "Deluxe Wish-A-World."

The Wish-A-World was secretly hooked up to the classroom computer. Marvin entered the name of any book in the school library and a page number, and one day later, whatever object or topic was being discussed on that page, anywhere in the world, would appear.

He tested it with the book *How Things Work*, page 46, about how pencils are made. In the morning his desk was stuffed with bright new yellow unsharpened pencils — enough for the whole school!

"Wonderful!" he blurted out in the middle of silent reading. Marvin could hardly believe it! Fortunately, no one paid any attention because everyone had come to accept Marvin's outbursts of strange behavior as normal for someone who seemed to spend as much time daydreaming as Marvin.

Marvin quickly got the encyclopedia and turned to "G." He was going to become rich overnight by materializing "gold." He hastily typed in the encyclopedia's name, volume number 7 and page 314, and set the machine to work. That night he hardly slept, bursting with excitement.

When Marvin got to school the next day, there was a giant commotion. Police cars, and ambulances filled the parking lot. Paramedics, the Red Cross, doctors, nurses, and scores of other people were rushing in and out of the school buildings. He thought there had been some sort of accident until he got closer and saw that inside the school were hundreds and hundreds of children from all over the world, dressed in every kind of clothing imaginable and speaking different languages. It was mass confusion!

In his haste to enter his request for "gold" Marvin had left out a digit in the page number. Instead of reading 314, it read 34, the page for "Children." There were so many children in the school that there was no room to walk! And the worst part of it was that over half of them were either starving or sick.

Teams of parents and community volunteers had been called to bring in food and water. Most of the hungry children were not even five-years old. Nurses were there to give them shots because many of the children were sick with diseases that kids in the United States rarely got anymore, and if they didn't get treatment fast, some were going to die!

Marvin was white as a sheet with fright! What had he done? After he figured out that his machine was somehow responsible for the mess, he thought of telling his teacher, but got scared when he heard the principal shout, "Who's responsible for this? They're in big trouble!"

The sick and hungry children were from the poor countries that made up over half of the world. Some of their homes had been bombed in wars. Others were poor because pollution or lack of rain had made it impossible for their families to grow food. And still others were from overcrowded cities where they had been sleeping in the street and begging.

It was pitiful and Marvin felt sick. Not only had he created problems for his school, the needs of these children seemed impossible to meet. And how would he ever send them back! The machine was only for getting things, not giving them back. Marvin thought he would be expelled from school for the next 100 years!

But as he watched, a strange thing happened. After the initial shock, people seemed to be happily working together. For all the trouble they went through to get food, medicine, and clothing for the children, they were enjoying themselves! And no one seemed mad! In fact, someone said, "We've got more than enough here. I'm glad these children can use it."

Marvin woke with a start. "What a dream!" he said to himself. He got dressed and ran to school without even having breakfast. As soon as the bell rang, he dashed into the room and turned off his machine. Luckily, he stopped it before anything appeared.

When the teacher began the social studies lesson for the day, Marvin raised his hand impatiently. "I've got a great idea," he said. "Why don't we make a project of studying how children live in other countries and maybe even raise some money to send them so they won't be so hungry!"

The class was stunned. Not only did Marvin rarely speak in class, he almost never made sense when he did.

"Good idea!" said the teacher with a puzzled look on his face. The class agreed.

Marvin's "Deluxe Wish-A-World" machine never did work after that, but he didn't care. Marvin got so involved in the project that he forgot about inventing crazy things. Instead, he invented more ways to help children all over the world get what *they* wished for.

Discussion Questions:

1. Why did Marvin turn off the machine before the gold appeared?
2. Why were most of the children hungry or sick? Name some of the countries the children may have come from.
3. Why didn't Marvin invent any more crazy things?
4. What made the class decide to accept Marvin's idea to study about and help children?
5. Why is it important to help others?
6. What are some ways that people can be of service to our community? ...to the nation? ...the world?
7. What would things be like if no one helped anyone else?

Marvin's Last Invention

Experience Sheet

Think about the story of Marvin, his inventions, and his dream. Then answer these questions:

1. **What did Marvin realize about the children of the world when he saw them in his dream? What made him want to help them?**

3. **How do you benefit personally from being of service to others? What do you get out of it?**

2. **Think of a time when you performed some kind of service for another person, a group, or the community. It could have been something as small as picking up some litter, or it could have been a major project. What did you do and how did you feel about it?**

New-Kid Survival Kits
A School Service Project

Objectives:

The children will:
— identify the needs and desires of new children.
— creatively compile information and services to meet the needs of new children.

Materials:

multiple copies of an appropriate organizer, e.g., inexpensive 3-ring binders, expandable file folders, large envelopes, presentation folders with pockets, etc.; art materials

Directions:

Begin this activity by asking the children: *What is it like to be a new kid at school or in an afterschool program? How many of you have had that experience?*

Invite volunteers to share what it's like to enter a new school or afterschool where you don't know anyone. Ask them if anyone showed them around during the first week or so, and whether or not the staff and children were welcoming and friendly. Point out that one of the nicest things they can do is to make a new child feel a part of the school from the very first day.

Announce that, as a service project, the children are going to prepare "survival kits" to give to new children.

Decide if it will be for the regular school or your afterschool program, and then as a total group, brainstorm the contents of the kit. Try to think of as many things as possible that a new child might find useful or encouraging.

Follow the rules of brainstorming, i.e., all suggestions are listened to, be creative, no evaluation during the brainstorming process, no put downs of any kind. Your list might include:

- a map of the school
- information about the school (description, history, unique characteristics, special relationships, e.g., with local colleges or businesses)
- a school district telephone directory (perhaps an abbreviated version)
- a school calendar, with special events marked
- a child handbook or list of rules/requirements
- information about teachers (names, classes, room numbers)
- information about office staff
- lists of sports, service groups, and clubs, with information on how they are organized and how to become involved
- descriptions of future events, including dates and times
- location of lost and found
- jokes, cartoons, or stories authored by children
- child-made coupons redeemable for special services, e.g., a campus tour, help with homework, introductions to six kids, a recess game partner, etc.
- a copy of the child newspaper
- PTA information
- a map of the town or city
- names and telephone numbers of local medical facilities
- coupons for treats at local stores and businesses
- information about public transportation
- a candy bar or treat

After the brainstorming process is concluded, go back and evaluate the list, narrow it down and make final selections.

Choose teams of volunteers to obtain or prepare the various items needed. When everything has been collected, appoint an "assembly team" to:

1. Decide on the best presentation of the items.
2. Put together a model kit
3. Design and produce a cover
3. Develop a system for efficiently assembling the kits.

Appoint another team to answer distribution questions. Have them consider the pros and cons of several distribution alternatives. For example:

- Assign a person to hand deliver each kit and perhaps act as a companion/guide throughout the first day.
- Mail the kit.
- Deliver the kit to the home of the new child.
- Give out kits at a monthly "newcomers" reception or party.

When the kits are finished and all of the decisions regarding distribution have been made, facilitate a culminating discussion.

Discussion Questions:

1. How do you feel when you do something to help a person you don't yet know?
2. How would you feel if a friendly child presented you with a kit like this when you entered a new school?
3. How do we benefit from reaching out to others?

Making Community Gift Basket

A Community Service Activity

Objectives:

The children will:
— identify the needs of local agencies.
— create and assemble gifts for others.

Materials:

a variety of gift items; suitable containers; wrapping and decorating materials

Directions:

Choose an appropriate local agency for which the children can make gift baskets. It might be a day-care facility, senior center, assisted-living home, or animal rescue agency. Preferably pick an organization that is local and for which it is possible for the children to do some research. Depending on the chosen agency, have the children find out such things as:

— the number of residents (children, seniors, animals)
— needs of the agency (Animal agencies might need old towels and blankets and donations of animal food. Day-care facilities may like gently used story books. Senior centers might be happy to have the children create letters and cards for each resident or come in and read to their residents.)
— whether the organization would welcome gifts (and perhaps visits) from the children
— the best times of the day for visits

As a group, choose the organization and determine what kinds of "gifts" the children would like to provide. Determine if it is best to prepare one large gift basket or several smaller or individual baskets for the organization. Decide what kind of container will best hold the contents of the gift baskets. You may use actual baskets or you may find that boxes, gift bags, or bags that the children decorate themselves work better.

Brainstorm with the children how they can collect the items for the baskets. Some ideas might be to circulate a flyer describing the project and listing needed items, sending a flyer home asking for donations of desired items. Perhaps the children would like to hold a fund-raiser (bake sale, car wash for staff members) to raise money to buy the items for the baskets. The basket items might include things belonging to the children that they can donate such as story books for young children.

Have teams of children assemble the gift baskets and wrap or decorate them. Make sure all the children participate in the preparation of the gift baskets. Determine the best way to deliver the baskets.

If an actual visit is possible, talk to the organization to find out what other activities the children can engage in during their visit. For example, they might:

— perform a skit
— lead some sing-a-longs
— play games
— lead simple stretching and movement exercises
— teach the young children or seniors a dance (wheelchairs can dance, too)

Prepare and practice with the children whatever activity it is that is planned, and discuss appropriate behavior.

After the baskets are delivered or the visit has been made, lead the children in a follow-up discussion.

Discussion Questions:

1. What was the best part of this activity for you?
2. How did giving to the seniors cause you to feel?
3. How do you think the recipients of the gift baskets felt?
4. Would you like to visit again? What ideas do you have for another visit?

I Helped Someone Who Needed and Wanted My Help

A Sharing Circle

Objectives:

The children will:
— distinguish between needing help and wanting it.
— site examples of giving personal service where it was needed.

Introduce the Topic:

Our topic today is, "I Helped Someone Who Needed and Wanted My Help." Sometimes a person needs help, but doesn't want it; other times a person wants help, but doesn't really need it. So let's talk about times when the help we gave was both needed and wanted.

Maybe you helped someone who was having a lot of trouble with a math problem. After working alone on the problem for quite some time, the person finally asked for your help. Or perhaps you saw someone struggling with a heavy load of boxes or bags. The person was clearly hurting from the weight of it, and was relieved when you offered to help. Or maybe your parent had a lot of work to do to get ready for company, and was grateful when you offered to take over some of the chores. Think it over for a few minutes. When you share, tell us how you knew that the person both needed and wanted your assistance. The topic is, "I Helped Someone Who Needed and Wanted My Help."

Discussion Questions:

1. What can happen if you insist on helping someone who doesn't want any help?
2. Why do we sometimes want help, even though we don't really need it?
3. How can you find out if a person wants your help?

What I Wish I Could Do to Make This a Better World

A Sharing Circle

Objectives:

The children will:
— identify global problems that need to be addressed.
— explain their relationship to the planet and all its people.

Introduce the Topic:

Our topic today allows us to think big and not worry about whether or not something is truly possible. We're going to talk about the way we <u>wish</u> things could be. The topic is, "What I Wish I Could Do to Make This a Better World."

If you could do anything you wished to make this a better world, what would it be? What would you give to the whole world? Maybe you'd give every kid a happy home with a loving family. Or maybe you'd send food to all the people who are hungry. Perhaps you'd give all people a good education so that they could be productive and successful. Maybe you'd make the world a better place by getting rid of pollution, or showing people how to settle conflicts peacefully, or giving everyone the ability to speak and understand many languages so they could communicate better. Or you might choose to make the world a better place by doing something fun. Use your imagination and tell us what you would do. The topic is, "What I Wish I Could Do to Make This a Better World."

Discussion Questions:

1. Which of our ideas might really be possible? How might they be accomplished?
2. Why is it important to think about the well being of the whole world? Why can't we just worry about ourselves?
3. What are some things that we can do to make the world a better place?

What Did You Learn About Service to Others?

Use this page to think about and record the things you have learned about service to others. You can write, draw pictures, scribble and doodle, create a poem, or anything else that has meaning to you and will help you remember what you have learned.

When you finish, show this page to someone else and explain what you have learned.

Tips for Teaching Service to Others:

♥ Create a family scrapbook of Service to Others. Use pictures in your album, add notes about the services performed, brochures where the service took place, thank you notes and anything else that is meaningful.

♥ Be an example yourself. If an elderly neighbor needs help with cleaning his yard, help him out. If someone with a handful of papers drops them, help in picking them up. Lead by what you do.

♥ Make it a family tradition to discuss at the dinner table how you helped someone out that day. Let your child brag about what was done and make sure you praise your child for all good acts, big or small.

♥ Ask your child to make a list of things he or she is grateful for. When you discuss the list, point out which items other boys and girls don't have. Help your child to feel special and grateful, and encourage him or her to help others who have much less.

Dear Parents,

In our Hearts and Minds group, your child has been discovering the joy of giving service to others. I encourage you to talk with your child about the rewards and impact of service that can come to both the giver and the receiver.

We started our unit with a story, Marvin's Last Invention. This is a story about a young boy who likes to experiment and invent things. His last invention, the Wish-A-World machine, started out good with the first try, but ended very differently on the second. Expecting to get gold from his wish machine, he got a surprise lesson in service to others instead. Marvin saw his school campus in total chaos with hundreds of needy children from all parts of the world. In the midst of the turmoil were police, paramedics, nurses, and hundreds of community volunteers who gathered together to help, thus turning the madness into a vision of great service to others. Ask your child to tell you about the story.

As a group, the children were involved in creating things that would be of direct benefit to others. In our Sharing Circles we talked about times we helped others, and also, ideas on how to make the world a better place. Ask you child to share some of his or her ideas with you. You'll be happy with what you hear.

Happy discussions together…

RESPONSIBILITY

— People need responsibility. They resist assuming it, but they cannot get along without it.

John Steinbeck

— The price of greatness is responsibility.

Winston Churchill

Vocabulary Words

- Fitfully
- Sheepishly
- Chatted
- Flickered
- Confrontation
- Pretending

Anna and the Silver Bracelet
by Dianne Schilling

"Hurry up, Lynette," said Anna impatiently. "The bell's about to ring. We'll be late, and Mr. Garcia will get grouchy."

"Okay, okay," replied Lynette, grabbing a paper towel from the holder in the corner. "I'm washing my hands — like a good girl."

Anna pushed through the door expecting Lynette to follow. But as she stepped into the sunshine, she heard Lynette — still in the bathroom — cry out, "Wow! Come look at this, Anna!"

Anna sighed and retraced her steps into the girl's bathroom. Lynette was still standing next to the towel holder. "Look what I found. It was on the floor behind the trash can," she exclaimed excitedly. She held up something shiny and silver. Anna couldn't tell what it was.

"Great," said Anna. "I'm going to class." With that she was out the door and heading down the outside hall at top speed. Lynette had to run to catch up.

"Isn't it beautiful?" Lynette said, juggling her pack with one hand while admiring the silver thing in the other.

"What is it?" asked Anna. She was more interested in reaching the classroom before the bell rang than looking at Lynette's treasure.

"A bracelet, silly. I think it's real silver."

"I wonder who lost it," said Anna, just as they reached the classroom door. "Whew, we made it."

The shrill bell sounded just as Anna turned the knob. She held the door so Lynette could enter, and watched her friend quickly shove the silver bracelet into a jeans pocket. Anna was surprised. Kids were supposed to turn in found items to their teacher or the office. Oh well, Lynette was probably waiting till later.

Jeff walked part way home with Anna and Lynette. He kept the girls in stitches with funny stories about the new puppies at his house. His mother was a breeder of Siberian Huskies, so daily Jeff had some new mischief to report.

As soon as Jeff turned down Tower Street and the two girls were climbing the hill to their own block, Lynette withdrew the silver bracelet from her pocket. She held it up so the sun reflected off the smooth metal. Then she let it slip down over her wrist and admired it against her skin.

"Why didn't you turn it in?" asked Anna, trying not to sound accusing.

"Oh, I don't know. Just forgot, I guess," said Lynette dreamily. A moment later she added, "But I will," before dropping the bracelet into her book pack.

As always, they reached Anna'a house first. Anna trudged up the walk and turned at the door to wave and watch as Lynette climbed the hill to her own home at the end of the street.

The next afternoon, as he did almost every afternoon, Mr. Garcia spent a few minutes reading aloud the office bulletin. The bulletin contained announcements about special events, changes in the school calendar, reminders of club meetings, and — occasionally — one or two lost-and-found items.

"A silver bracelet with an engraved flower design was lost at school on Tuesday. If you find it or have any information, talk to the secretary, Mrs. Peterson," read Mr. Garcia.

Anna shot a questioning look at Lynette who was working quietly in the back of the room. Lynette didn't look up.

When Mr. Garcia finished the bulletin, he moved right into a social studies lesson, and then a writing assignment, and then cooperative group projects. Anna wanted to talk to Lynette about the bracelet, but she never had a chance. After school she waited by the elm tree at the corner of the playground, but Lynette never showed up, so Anna walked home alone.

Anna had trouble concentrating on her homework. Images of the shiny silver bracelet kept popping into her mind. Mostly she thought about the bracelet on her friend's wrist. Lynette loved jewelry and it was easy to see she was crazy about that bracelet. Was she planning to keep it?

Anna decided to find out. Feeling nervous but determined, she went to the kitchen phone, picked up the handset and punched in Lynette's number. Lynette's brother answered and called to his sister. When she picked up the phone, Lynette sounded breathless and cheerful. "Hi, sorry you had to walk home alone. I forgot to tell you my mom was picking me up for a dentist appointment."

"Yuck," said Anna, with a shiver. "The last time I went to the dentist I had to have two fillings. I hate that awful sound, and the shots hurt. Did you have to have shots?" The purpose of Anna's call was momentarily washed beneath a wave of sympathy.

"No," said Lynette. "But I don't like it either, and anyway let's not talk about dentists. Wasn't Henry funny at lunch today? I wish he could be in our class."

The girls talked about their friends and boys and family outings. Finally Anna remembered why she called and asked, "Lynette, did you turn in the bracelet?"

Silence.

"Lynette? Are you there?"

Finally, her voice shaking, Lynette said slowly, "Anna, I told you I was going to turn it in. Just don't bug me about it, okay?"

"But have you turned it in?" persisted Anna.

"No, not yet. I keep forgetting. What's the matter, don't you trust me? Anyway, it's none of your business!" Now Lynette's voice sounded angry.

"But it doesn't belong to you Lynette, and somebody feels bad because it's gone. How would you feel if..."

Anna heard a 'click' and realized that Lynette had hung up. She felt awful and wondered if she was being a bad friend. She thought about calling Lynette back and apologizing, but decided against it. Maybe she should just mind her own business.

But minding her own business was tough for Anna. Especially when "lost bracelet" posters began to show up around school. She saw one on a bulletin board outside the main office and another taped to the side of a classroom building. She practically ran into one stapled to a utility pole on the edge of the playground.

The more she thought about it, the more Anna realized that the lost bracelet was her business. After all, she was there when Lynette found it. She saw Lynette put the bracelet in her pocket. And Lynette was her best friend — though, come to think of it, she wasn't acting very friendly these days.

A couple of afternoons later during recess, Anna and Lynette were playing on the bars with several other girls, when someone mentioned the lost bracelet.

"My mom won't let me wear my nice stuff to school," said one girl, "It's too easy to lose."

"Yea, and who's going to turn in a bracelet like that? Most kids would keep it," said another.

"Finders keepers, losers weepers," chanted Lynette. The other girls laughed.

Anna couldn't believe her ears. Lynette really did plan to keep the bracelet, and not only that — she thought it was okay! Right then and there, Anna made up her mind to visit the school counselor.

Ms. Elliott was one of Anna's favorite people at school. She was friendly and helpful, and when Anna's grandfather died last year, Ms. Elliott and Anna talked several times, sometimes taking long walks around the neighborhood near the school.

When Anna knocked on the side of her open office door, Ms. Elliott looked up and smiled brightly. "Hi, Anna," she said. "Come in and sit down. I haven't had a visit from you in a long time. I hear you're doing well in class. Why don't you bring me up to date."

They chatted about school and about Anna's family. Anna felt nervous and the pleasant conversation calmed her. After a few minutes, Ms. Elliott paused and asked, "Did you have a special reason for dropping by today, Anna?" Anna nodded and stared at the floor. Ms. Elliott waited.

Finally, Anna blurted out, "I know who has the lost bracelet. I saw her pick it up off the floor of the bathroom and put in her pocket. I don't think she's going to turn it in."

Anna told Ms. Elliott the whole story. She explained that keeping the secret was making her feel bad, and she expressed her confusion over what to do. She wanted to be loyal to her best friend, but didn't think it was right for Lynette to keep something that didn't belong to her. Ms. Elliott listened. She let Anna know that she understood how hard it was to tell on a friend. In the end, though, Ms. Elliott stressed that Anna was feeling badly because she was going against her own conscience.

"Pretending you don't know anything about the bracelet is not a responsible thing to do," said Ms. Elliott seriously. "Your conscience won't let you be like an ostrich who sticks her head in the sand. It wants you to be a responsible person, and there are only two ways to do that. Either convince Lynette that she must return the bracelet, or report what you know."

"But Lynette will hate me," worried Anna.

"Maybe not," said Ms. Elliott. "You don't know how Lynette really feels about keeping the bracelet. I'll bet that deep down, she has just as many doubts as you."

Anna felt better when she left Ms. Elliott's office. She decided to try that afternoon, one more time, to talk some sense into Lynette.

But when Jeff turned off at Tower Street and the two girls were climbing the hill, Anna didn't know how to begin her confrontation, so she said instead, "That's a cool jacket, Lynette. Is it new?"

"Isn't it great! My dad bought it for me on a business trip. Everybody kept coming up to me all day, telling me how much they liked it. It's the neatest jacket I've ever had!" exclaimed Lynette, proudly.

A little light bulb flickered in Anna's brain. "You probably shouldn't wear it to school," she said, watching Lynette's reaction.

"Why not? shrugged Lynette, "It's been cold lately."

Anna focused on the sidewalk and tried to speak casually. "Because if you ever lay it on a bench, or hang it over the back of a chair in the cafeteria, or leave it on a hook in the bathroom, you'll probably never see it again."

Lynette's steps slowed, but she didn't say anything, so Anna plunged ahead.

"Whoever finds it will think it's cool and keep it," she said.

"They wouldn't do that," protested Lynette.

"Sure they will. They'll say 'finders keepers' and they won't worry about you at all," insisted Anna.

Suddenly Lynette stopped. "I know why you're saying this to me, Anna, and it's a mean thing to do. You're hoping someone will take my jacket because of the bracelet. If you care so much about that old bracelet, why don't you find out who lost it and be her friend! I don't want you for a friend anymore!"

Anna stood alone at her front gate, watching Lynette storm up the hill. She felt sad and fought the urge to cry.

The sadness grew as afternoon turned to evening and smells of dinner drifted through the house. Anna wasn't hungry. She knew she was going to have to tell on Lynette and it made her feel queasy. She picked her way through the meal, trying to act normal, did her homework and slept fitfully.

Anna didn't expect to see Lynette the next morning, so she was surprised when her "ex-friend" showed up at the front gate 15 minutes earlier than usual. Nervously, Anna walked to the gate. "Hi," she said. "I didn't think you'd want to walk together today, and anyway I'm not quite ready." Anna noticed that Lynette was not wearing her new jacket. She was wearing the silver bracelet.

"I'm sorry about yesterday," said Lynette sheepishly. "I thought about what you said all night. I realized that if someone found my jacket and kept it, I'd think they were the worst person in the world. The more I thought about it, the more I felt like the worst person in the world."

Anna was so relieved her knees started to shake.

Lynette took off the bracelet and held it out to Anna. "Here," she said. "Take it. I never really wanted it. ...Well, maybe I did at first, but not for long. Will you turn it in for me?"

Anna shook her head firmly. "No, Lynette," she said, "you have to do it. You were the one who found it and you were the one who kept it all this time, so you're the one who has to turn it in."

"But I'm scared," pleaded Lynette. "That's why I didn't take it back. I was just admiring it in my drawer, and I kept putting it off. Then after a few days I couldn't take it back because it would look like I was planning to keep it. It's really stupid, but I don't know how to explain it!"

"You can say exactly what you said to me," suggested Anna. "I talked to Ms. Elliott about it, and she said we'll feel better if we take responsibility for our actions. I think she's right."

"We?" questioned Lynette.

"Yes, we," repeated Anna. "I knew you had the bracelet all this time, and I didn't say anything until I talked to Ms. Elliott. Of course, she didn't report it. She's a counselor. She just put it back on me. So I have to go with you and take responsibility for playing dumb."

"Really? You'll go with me?" said Lynette hopefully.

"Sure," said Anna. "You'll see, — it won't be so bad. Wait while I get my things and we'll go do it right now."

Anna ran in the house and was back in less than two minutes, breathlessly stumbling through the gate. The two friends threw their arms around each other and hugged. Laughing, they headed down the hill.

"Come on," said Lynette. "Let's get this over with!"

Discussion Questions:

1. What's wrong with keeping a lost item that you happen to find?
2. Why did Lynette wait to turn in the bracelet?
3. Why was she afraid to turn it in later?
4. Why did Anna feel that turning in the bracelet was her responsibility, too?
5. What does it mean to be a responsible person?
6. What does it mean to take responsibility for your actions?

Anna and the Silver Bracelet

Experience Sheet

Think about the story of Anna, whose friend found a bracelet and almost kept it. Write your answers to these questions:

1. Have you ever lost something and gotten it back because the person who found it was responsible and honest? Describe what happened:

2. Have you ever found something and turned it in? Why did you turn in the item, and how did you feel about your actions?

3. You've probably heard the saying, "Finders keepers, losers weepers." Maybe you've even said it yourself. What's wrong with the ideas behind that saying?

Framing the Blame Game

Cartooning and Discussion

Objectives:

The children will:
— describe situations involving denial of responsibility or blaming.
— explain the importance and benefits of accepting responsibility for their actions.
— creatively demonstrate the contrast between blaming and being responsible in specific situations.

Materials:

drawing paper; colored markers, pencils, or crayons; sample cartoon strips clipped from the newspaper or taken off the internet

Directions:

Begin by asking the children how they feel when they get blamed for something they didn't do. Listen to their responses, and then ask: *Have you ever been in a situation where a person has done something wrong or made a mistake, and you know it, but the person denies it?*

Point out that when we deny responsibility for our actions, we are in effect blaming someone else — even if we don't actually point a finger at someone and say "she did it."

Give the children several examples of blaming and elicit many more from them. Here are some possibilities:

- A child with frosting on his or her face denies having eaten a piece of cake.
- A child fails a test and says the teacher is stupid or unfair.

- A man has a car accident and blames his wife because she was talking and taking his attention away from the road.
- A person is late for work and blames the heavy traffic.
- A teenager breaks his mother's favorite vase and says that it shouldn't have been so close to the edge of the shelf.
- A batter keeps missing the ball and claims the pitcher is lousy, the sun is in his eyes, and the spectators are making him nervous.
- A child is caught shoplifting and tells her mother, "The other kids made me do it."

Announce that the children are going to make pairs of cartoon strips, one showing a blaming situation, and the other showing the same situation but with the "guilty" character accepting responsibility in the last frame. Show and read aloud the sample cartoon strips to the children. Explain that these cartoons are models they can use to see how a cartoon is depicted in a very simple way in each frame.

Distribute the art materials. Suggest that the children illustrate a situation from their own experience, or one that was mentioned in the earlier class discussion. Remind the children not to use real names. Stipulate that each cartoon strip should have at least three frames, showing:

1. the incident (mistake or wrongdoing)
2. the decision concerning what to do (showing fear, guilt, confusion, inner struggle, etc.)
3. blaming/denying or acceptance of responsibility

Children whose situations require additional frames should be urged to limit the number to a maximum of six.

When the cartoons are finished, post them on a bulletin board. As a group, look at and discuss each pair of cartoons, giving praise and feedback to the artist. Spread this process over several days, if necessary, facilitating discussion during each session.

Discussion Questions:

1. Why is it hard to admit when you are wrong?
2. When you make a mess, whose job is it to clean it up? Why?
3. Does anyone ever really make you do something? Explain.
4. How do we benefit by admitting our mistakes and taking responsibility?
5. What are some of the things that can happen if we don't accept responsibility?
6. What have you learned from this activity?

Variation:

Instead of making cartoons (or as an alternative for some children), allow teams to develop two skits, one dramatizing a blaming situation and the other showing the same situation with the character accepting responsibility.

Note:

An excellent internet resource for using comics with children is *www.makebeliefscomix.com*.

Striving for Excellence
Skits and Discussion

Objectives:

The children will:
— describe times when they did their best.
— creatively demonstrate what can happen when individuals don't do their best.
— explain the costs and benefits of pursuing excellence.

Directions:

Ask the children to think of a time when they did their very best at something — absolutely the most thorough, skillful, quality job they could do at the time. Tell them that this effort could have been made toward something very big and important or something relatively small. Emphasize that what you're after is the quality of the effort, not the importance of the end product. Suggest that the effort could have been made toward the accomplishment of such things as:

- a school project
- a game or athletic event
- a single moment in an athletic event (like a particular time at bat)
- a household chore
- baking a cake or preparing a salad
- drawing a picture
- wrapping a present
- performing in a dance or music recital
- a spelling test or spelling bee

Invite several children to briefly share their incident with the class. Be sure to ask these volunteers how they felt about themselves for doing their best — and how other people felt about them. Introduce the concept of *excellence*, and talk about developing a habit of striving for excellence in every pursuit.

Write the following list on the board:

airline pilot	school bus driver
ball player	ballet dancer
fire fighter	doctor
architect or builder	baby-sitter
chef/cook	automobile mechanic
movie or TV actor	crossing guard

Have the children form groups of three or four. Announce that each group is going to develop a skit showing what can happen if one of the people listed on the board slacks off and doesn't do his or her best.

Have each group select a recorder and choose a job or profession from the list (avoiding duplications). Suggest that the groups begin by describing a specific job that their subject might be doing, and then brainstorming possible consequences of the person's not doing his or her best. This process should give the groups plenty of material for a skit. Once their scenario is established, have them assign roles and rehearse.

One at a time, have the groups perform their completed skits for the entire class. After each skit, facilitate a brief discussion, focusing on the importance of doing one's best.

Discussion Questions:

1. Who benefits when we do our best?
2. How do you know when you are doing your best?
3. What does it cost to do your best? What, if anything, do you have to give up?
4. Does striving for excellence build good character? How?

A Time I Helped Without Being Asked
A Sharing Circle

Objectives:

The children will:
— describe the difference between choosing to do something and being told to do it.
— state the importance of assuming responsibility for things that need to be done.

Introduce the Topic:

Today we're going to talk about taking the initiative — about accepting responsibility without being told to by an adult. Our topic is, "A Time I Helped Without Being Asked."

Think of a time when something that needed to be done and took it upon yourself to do it. No one had to tell you or ask you or even hint to you that it needed doing. Maybe you walked into the kitchen and saw a sink full of dirty dishes and, instead of just ignoring it, you cleaned it up. Or maybe you saw someone break something and you helped pick up the pieces. Perhaps a neighbor was searching the street for a missing pet and you joined in. Or you might have stayed to help a teacher straighten up a classroom after school. You can probably think of lots of times when you decided on your own to take responsibility. Tell us about one of those times. The topic is, "A Time I Helped Without Being Asked."

Discussion Questions:

1. How did you feel when you helped without being asked?
2. How would your feelings have been different if you had been asked, or even ordered, to do the same thing?
3. What does it mean to be a responsible person?
4. Why is it important for each of us to take responsibility for things that need to be done?

A Time I "Took My Medicine"

A Sharing Circle

Objectives:

The children will:
— explain the connection between an action and its consequences.
— describe how they benefit by taking responsibility for their mistakes.

Introduce the Topic:

Have you ever heard the expression, "take your medicine?" It means that when you do something wrong or make a mistake, you have to be ready to take the consequences. Today we're going to talk about times when we accepted our medicine because we knew we deserved it. The topic is, "A Time I 'Took My Medicine.'"

Think of a time when you did something wrong or against the rules, or simply made a bad mistake. It doesn't matter whether you did it on purpose or accidentally. In either case, you accepted the consequences without whining, or making excuses, or blaming someone else. Maybe you were punished for going somewhere that you parents told you not to go, or perhaps you had too many fouls in basketball and had to leave the game. Maybe you didn't do your homework or finish a report on time, and accepted a failing grade without grumbling about it. Or perhaps you were put on restriction for lying, fighting, or getting a bad report card. Think about it for a few moments. The topic is, "A Time I 'Took My Medicine.'"

Discussion Questions:

1. Why is it better to accept the consequences of your actions instead of trying to get away with something wrong?
2. What would it be like if everyone tried to get away with breaking the rules and doing bad things?
3. Does it take courage to admit your mistakes and take the consequences? Explain.
4. How can admitting your mistakes and taking your medicine make you a better person?

What Did You Learn About Responsibility?

Use this page to think about and record the things you have learned about responsibility. You can write, draw pictures, scribble and doodle, create a poem, or anything else that has meaning to you and will help you remember what you have learned.

When you finish, show this page to someone else and explain what you have learned.

Tips for Teaching Responsibility:

♡ We all want our children to act responsibly because they want to, not just because they are told to. Explain how a football team (or any team) needs more than one great player to win games. In the same way your family needs everyone's contribution to run smoothly and well. Talk about the various roles each family member plays and how everyone's help and contribution is important. Be sure to praise your child for being responsible and for doing his or her part in the family.

———

♡ Age-appropriate chores are a simple way to teach your child responsibility, and letting your child make some of his or her own choices will help teach responsibility and accountability.

———

♡ Being a responsible adult sets a good example for your child's watchful eyes. Following through with what you say, keeping a promise, or being on time are ways you can set good examples.

Dear Parents

In our Hearts and Minds group the children have discussed and discovered what it means to be responsible for their actions. We considered not only taking or not taking responsibility, but we also recognized the difference between blaming others and being responsible for our actions.

Our story, Anna and the Silver Bracelet, is about two friends, Anna and Lynette. One day at school Lynette found a beautiful silver bracelet in the girl's bathroom. Anna knew about it and was waiting for her friend to turn it in to the lost and found. After several days and lots of lost posters all around school, Anna could see that turning in the bracelet was not going to happen. As the story continued, we discovered why Anna was feeling uncomfortable about her friend's behavior, as well as her own, and discovered how to handle the situation.

Some awesome ideas were discussed during our Sharing Circles where we talked about accepting responsibility without being told to!

In our other activities we learned more about taking responsibility and doing our best.

I encourage you to ask, "What did you learn today?" And be pleased with how your child responds.

Happy talking together…

SELF-CONTROL

— The greatest conflicts are not between two people but between one person and himself.

Garth Brooks

— Whenever you're in conflict with someone, there is one factor that can make the difference between damaging your relationship and deepening it. That factor is attitude.

Timothy Bentley

Vocabulary Words

- Irritable
- Careened
- Drawl
- Contraption
- Pivoting
- Claim

An Alterna-Tive Tale
by Dianne Schilling

The Want family lived in a big, sturdy house with a yard the size of a small park on a quiet street in the town of Amity.

It was a good thing that the house was big, because fully sixteen Wants ranging in age from eighteen months to 73 years lived within its walls. It was an even better thing that the walls were thick and sturdy, because the Wants tended to be — well, *loud* probably says it best. And it was indeed fortunate that the yard was deep enough to keep the house well back from the quiet street — or it would not have been quiet at all.

The reason for all the noise in the Want house can be summed up in one word — *confusion*. It wasn't that the Wants didn't love one another — they did. But they were active, independent people and it seemed as though every Want always wanted something different from every other Want.

For example, at around seven o'clock each weekday morning, approximately thirteen hungry, hurrying Wants would arrive in the kitchen eager for breakfast. These were the family members who needed to leave for work or school. They were always rushed and often irritable. If four of them wanted eggs, you could be sure that only one preferred scrambled, while the other three insisted on fried, poached, and boiled. Assuming they were lucky enough to find four pans and fit them on the four burners of the stove, this left no room for the Wants who hurried in wanting to fix oatmeal, french toast, pancakes, or to boil water for tea.

At nine o'clock at night, cries went up for more different TV shows than there were channels to choose from. And on Saturday morning, at least nine or ten Wants would claim to need one of the family's two cars for errands or activities that had absolutely no relation in time or location to one another.

The only time two Wants ever wanted the same thing was when there was only one of it. For instance, Wilbur and Winnifred could always be counted on to want the washing machine at the same hour of the same day. And if there was only one light bulb left, at least five desktop or bedside reading lamps would blow out at virtually the same instant. You can probably imagine how it was in the Want house. Arguments, yelling, endless discussions, and very few decisions. Rarely could people agree on who should go to the store and buy the groceries. Or what groceries ought to be bought. Or how they ought to be prepared. There were always sixteen different ideas about where the Christmas tree should be placed, and eleven volunteers who wanted to put the angel on the top of the tree.

Visiting home from college one weekend, Wanda Want (who was studying business management) said, "What this family needs most is a household manager. Maybe then some decisions would get made."

This suggestion was followed by a loud and lively discussion among several members of the family. Everyone had a slightly different viewpoint, and everyone expressed it. Of course, no agreements were reached so no decisions were made. Wiley and Wilomena went off to the kitchen table and tried to write a want ad — together. They argued about it for hours. They couldn't agree on what a household manager should do. They couldn't even decide how many lines to write, or where to place the ad, or when to stop arguing and eat lunch.

Finally, Wanda wrote the ad herself. She was smart enough not to ask for anyone else's ideas or reactions. But when it appeared in the newspaper, she cut it out and posted it on the front of the refrigerator for everyone to see:

Full-time Household Manager wanted for very large, active family. Cooking and cleaning not required. Must know how to promote self-control, conflict resolution, and decision making. Call 756-8742 weekdays after 7:00 p.m. and ask for Wanda.

The phone number was for Wanda's college dormitory. For the next two weeks, Wanda conducted interviews during the week. When she came home on the first Friday night, she refused to discuss the progress of her plan with any member of the family. But when she came home at the end of the second week, Wanda made an announcement. She said, "Tomorrow morning at 10:00 a.m., the Want Family Household Manager will arrive for her first day of work. I would like all of you to be present." Then, without another word, she climbed the stairs to her room.

On Saturday morning at exactly 10:00 a.m., the doorbell rang. For one glorious moment, every activity, every discussion, and every argument stopped. The Want house was silent.

Then it exploded. Dishes and pans clattered into the sink, chair legs scraped across the floor and doors in every corner of the house swung open and slammed shut. The sound of running, walking and scuffling footsteps mixed with whispered chatter, yelling and laughter as everyone hurried to the door.

A collision was inevitable. Weld and Wendy slid into the entryway and dove for the door as if it were first base at a Little League game. William dove for the door from halfway up the entry staircase, and Winter careened down the hall on her skateboard. There was a loud crash. The front door shuddered and rattled on its hinges — then burst open to reveal four young Wants in a heap on the floor surrounded by a curious (and curious-looking) crowd of twelve onlookers.

Leaning against the porch railing was a tall, angular woman with black hair and knowing dark eyes. Her arms were folded loosely across the front of a bright yellow warm-up suit. A smile of amusement played at one corner of her broad mouth. Leaning on its end against the railing next to the women was a long leather carrying case that almost equaled her in height.

The woman watched with interest as Weld, Wendy, William and Winter untangled themselves. Then she picked up her carrying case and stepped through the door without being asked. Breaking a path across the entryway, the woman walked briskly to the living room and stopped.

"My name is Alterna," she said, pivoting smoothly to survey her audience. "Alterna Tive." Alterna looked steadily into sixteen pairs of eyes — one pair at a time. A grin traveled back and forth between her large ears. "Rhymes with jive," she added in an exaggerated drawl.

Everyone stared, speechless. Then Wanda stepped forward. "Welcome Alterna," she said, extending her hand. "Allow me to introduce my family." Wanda moved down the line and Alterna followed her, shaking hands and repeating each person's name. "Weston, Wisteria, Wooley, Walter..."

When the introductions were over, Alterna stepped back and asked cheerfully, "Well, what's everybody doing today?"

"Shopping!"

"Homework!"

"Little League!"

"The lake!"

"Weston can't go fishing 'til he mows the lawn," said Winter, loudly.

"It's not my turn," yelled Weston. "It's yours, and you know it!"

"I did it last week."

"Well, somebody else will have to do it then, because I get stuck with that job all the time," Weston said firmly.

Alterna was unzipping her carrying case. She reached in and lifted out a leggy metal contraption and, with a few pulls and snaps, transformed it into an easel. Then she unrolled a pad of paper and hung it from the top of the easel. A fat, black pen appeared in her hand.

"It's a big yard," observed Alterna, holding up her hand to quiet the group. "I bet that when you do the yard work, it takes you all day."

Nodding heads — and groans.

"If you've done yard work even once during the last year, come up here and sign your name," said Alterna, tossing her pen to Weston.

Two minutes later, the chart had nine names on it.

"Hey, look at what you just did," exclaimed Alterna. "There was only one pen and you took turns using it. And I didn't even have to tell you to!"

Shrugs and giggles.

Alterna studied the list. "So, this is the yard team," she said. "Is there anyone else who would like to be on the yard team?"

Seven-year-old Woody stepped forward. "Me," he announced. Alterna gave him the pen and he signed his name.

"Let's see," said Alterna, "we have one big yard, and one big team with ten individual members. How many ways can a team of ten make sure that the yard gets cleaned every week?"

"Take turns."

"Make a schedule."

"Do it together."

"Divide up the work."

"Divide up the yard."

"Have two teams of five, and appoint judges to decide which team did the best work."

"Or the fastest!"

"And award a prize!"

Alterna was writing all the ideas down on a clean sheet of paper. "Tell you what," she smiled. "I think the team has some terrific ideas. And I think the team can find a solution to the problem without the rest of us hanging around. Weston, since you seem to have the most yard experience, you're in charge of this meeting. Here's the pen — and here are the rules."

Alterna looked from one team member to another. "Only one person talks at a time. Everybody else listens. Keep listing ideas until you run out of them. Then use the ideas to create a solution. The solution doesn't have to be perfect, but it has to be one that every member of the team will agree to try for at least two weeks. No exceptions. Okay? We'll check back with you later."

Alterna went with the rest of the family into the kitchen. "I could sure use a cup of tea," she said. "Do you have any?"

"I'll fix it," offered Wayne.

"No, let me do it," begged Wilomena.

They began to struggle over the tea kettle.

"Hold it!" cried Alterna. "Let me have the kettle for a second."

Alterna shook the tea kettle to make certain it was empty and then placed it on the floor and gave it a spin. "When it stops, the person closest to where the spout is pointing gets to make the tea. And since I drink a lot of tea, the other person gets to make it next time."

Wayne won the spin. He fixed spicy orange tea for everyone.

Throughout the day, Alterna Tive migrated from one part of the house to another, watching the Wants closely, and jumping in whenever an argument erupted, which of course was often. When a conflict was complicated, Alterna used her easel. Most of the time, she just used her head.

"Where do you think you're going with those car keys," demanded Wilbur. He was chasing Wysteria down the hall.

"I have to pick up Wendy and Weld from Little League practice," called Wysteria over her shoulder. She quickened her pace.

"You don't have to leave yet. The practice isn't over for another hour," shouted Wilbur. "I was just about to run over to the building-supply store."

"There's a sale on sheets at the department store. I have to stop there first."

Wysteria was out the door, with Wilbur in hot pursuit. "I won't be able to fix the screen door today," insisted Wilbur.

"Wilbur, I have to go now because this is the last day of the sale. Why can't you just wait till I get back."

"Because it will be too late," shouted Wilbur in reply. "I have to fix the screen before dark."

Wysteria lifted the garage door. "No you don't. It's been broken for a month. Another day won't hurt."

"I don't want to wait another day! I want to do it today!"

The battle was broken by the blare of the car horn. When she had captured their attention, Alterna pulled her arm from the driver's window of the car and stepped out of the garage. "My goodness," she scolded. "Two smart people putting all their energy into fighting over one car. Why don't you put your energy into finding a way to share the car and accomplish all three errands — the sheets, the building supplies, and the Little League pick up."

Wilbur stared at the ground and grumbled. Wysteria looked embarrassed. "Maybe you could pick up the kids," she said. "After you get your supplies." Wysteria offered Wilbur the car keys.

"Yeah, I could do that, but then you'd miss the sheet sale."

"No," said Wysteria. "I could go after you get back."

"Or I could drop you off at the department store first, and pick you up after I pick up Weld and Wendy," suggested Wilbur.

"That might be better," said Wysteria. "Come on. Let's not waste any more time."

Alterna stayed for dinner. Between the pasta and the pie, she made an announcement. "Before I leave tonight," she said. "I am going to appoint two people to be systems managers for the next week. My experience has taught me that a lot of conflicts can be avoided if you take the time to set things up right from the beginning. For example, a systems manager might design a car-use schedule and post it near the door. People who wanted to use one of the cars would sign for it in advance. Another thing a systems manager might do is notice when the family is running out of something that everybody uses — like shampoo or bananas — and put that item on the shopping list. As a systems manager, your job is to pay attention to the kinds of conflicts people have, and then try to figure out ways of preventing them."

All but two Wants immediately applied for the position of systems manager. "I have fourteen applicants for two jobs," said Alterna. She paused for several seconds and then asked matter-of-factly, "Who would be willing to withdraw his or her application and wait till another week?"

Three Wants withdrew.

"That leaves eleven applicants for two jobs," said Alterna patiently. "You know, if they want to, systems managers can ask for advice and suggestions. Maybe some of you would be willing to serve as advisors this week — if you're asked to that is."

Seven more Wants withdrew their applications.

"That leaves four applicants for two jobs," said Alterna. "I need two more withdrawals."

"Wait a minute," chimed in Walter. "Who says that a job has to be for just one person? Why can't each job be filled by a team of two?"

A chorus of approval sounded from around the dining table. Alterna grinned and gestured her thumbs-up approval. "Now you're really getting the idea!" she laughed.

"Alterna," asked little Wooley. "Are you coming back every Saturday?"

"I think two or three more Saturdays will be enough," replied Alterna. "After that, you won't need me anymore. In my business," smiled Alterna broadly, "short-term employment is a sign of success."

Discussion Questions:

1. What are some examples of self-control that you heard in this story? When did the characters show a lack of self-control?
2. Why is it important for only one person to talk at a time when you are trying to solve a problem?
3. Why did Alterna tell the yard team that its solution for doing yard work didn't have to be perfect?
4. Spinning the kettle on the floor was a game of chance. What are some other games of chance that can be used to settle conflicts?
5. How can we keep from getting locked into seeing just one solution — our own?
6. If Warren and Wanda hadn't been able to move the computer, what else could they have done?
7. Why do you think Wysteria was embarrassed when Alterna found her and Wilbur fighting over the car?
8. What did Alterna do to help the 14 applicants avoid a conflict over the systems manager job?

An Alterna-Tive Tale
Experience Sheet

What did you learn about self-control from the story of the Want family? What did you learn about solving conflicts? Think about the story as you answer these questions:

1. Write about a time when you had to really demonstrate self-control. What happened, and what did you do?

2. Think of a conflict you have had with someone. Are there ways that conflict could have been prevented? If so, how? If not, why?

3. Alterna Tive got her name from the word alternative. It's a perfect name for her. Can you explain why?

A Wave of Self-Control
Game and Discussion

Objectives:

The children will:
— spontaneously complete sentences related to self-control
— identify do's and don'ts related to self-control.
— describe how having specific behavioral goals can lead to greater self-control.

Materials:

whiteboard or chart paper

Directions:

Have the children sit in one large circle. Pick a sentence starter from the list below. "Send" the starter quickly around the circle like a wave. Have each child in turn rise, tack an ending on the sentence, and sit back down. At times you might want to send the same starter around two or three times. Or begin a second starter immediately after the first one passes the last person.

Sentence Starters

- When I'm angry at someone, I usually...
- A good way to control my temper is to...
- A rule I have trouble following is...
- Self-control is important because...
- I sometimes get in trouble for...
- I get impatient about...
- I don't like waiting for...
- I'm getting better about controlling...
- When I feel impatient, I...
- A good way to blow off steam is...

After the game, point out that all of the sentence starters had to do with self-control. (Or ask the children to guess the central theme.)

Explain that having self-control is part of being a responsible person. If you have self-control, you are able to *restrain* and *regulate* your own behavior. Ask the children to name some *do's* and *don'ts* associated with self-control. Write their suggestions on the board, creating lists that contain items like these:

DO:

    raise your hand
    wait your turn
    sit quietly
    be polite
    have consideration
    be patient
    show respect for others
    be understanding

DON'T:

    fidget
    interrupt
    lose your temper
    throw things
    scream
    hit others
    use bad language.

Next, ask the children how they might go about changing their behavior and gaining more self-control. Listen to their suggestions, and write these steps on the board:

1. Decide exactly what behavior you want to change.
2. Set a self-control goal.
3. Think of things you can do, or not do, to help yourself reach your goal.
4. Keep working on the new behavior, little by little, until it becomes a habit.

Give the children an example like this one:

Rick had a hard time keeping his room clean. He set a goal to develop the habit of picking up his things every morning before school and every evening at bedtime. Since he shared the room with his younger brother, Mike, Rick had to enlist Mike's cooperation. He decided to organize the closet and the shelves so that his books, toys, and other gear were kept separate from Mike's. When Mike left things lying around, Rick would ask nicely, "Please pick that up — I'm working on my goal." Each day he spent a little time doing the tasks that needed to be done, and eventually his parents no longer had to scold him about keeping his room clean. He had achieved his goal!

Conclude the activity with further discussion.

Discussion Questions:

1. How much self-control do babies have?
2. Do you think people gain more self-control as they grow up? Why or why not?
3. Is gaining self-control as you get older automatic, or do you have to work at it? Explain.
4. Over what behavior would you like to have more control?

Extension:

Use this activity as a springboard to helping individual children set self-control goals. Work through this goal-setting process with the children on a one-to-one basis. Draw and duplicate a picture of a target on a sheet of paper. Within the target make a number of concentric circles. Every day that a child shows progress toward his or her individual self-control goal (which should be written on the sheet), allow the child to color in one of the circles, starting with the outside edge of the target and working toward the center. Use many different colors. When the entire target is filled in, congratulate the child for reaching his or her goal.

Control Yourself
Discussion and Informal Self-Assessment

Objectives:

The children will:
— describe examples of self-control and self-management.
— demonstrate behaviors associated with self-control
— affirm themselves for their own levels of self-control.

Materials:

whiteboard

Directions:

Begin this session by asking the children what the term *self-control* means. Listen to and reflect the children's responses. In the process, establish that having self-control means being able to *restrain* and regulate one's own behavior. It means not losing your temper, not throwing things, not screaming, hitting others, or using bad language. Then say: *Think of a time when your emotions were so strong that you couldn't control yourself. Maybe you didn't want to cry or yell or laugh, but the feelings were overpowering.*

Invite volunteers to tell the group about their experiences. Ask one or two to act out their incidents, demonstrating exactly what happened.

Next, whisper one of the following situations to a volunteer and have that child act out the situation in pantomime (nonverbally). Have the group guess what is happening and identify the emotion that the child is trying to control.

— *You just crashed your bike, banging your leg badly, in front of several older kids.*

— *You get back a paper that you worked very hard on. It's covered with red marks and graded C-.*
— *Walking home at dusk, you turn a corner and practically run right into a big skunk.*
— *While your teacher is explaining an assignment, you see another child do something hysterically funny and you try to keep from breaking up.*
— *Your parent restricts you for something your brother or sister did.*
— *You are walking home alone after just learning that a boy or girl you have a crush on likes you too.*

Repeat this process with the remainder of the situations and a new volunteer each time. After each pantomime, talk about methods typically used to control reactions to various emotions (biting tongue, clenching fists, taking deep breaths, blinking, stiffening muscles, looking away, etc.)

Draw a long horizontal line across the board. At one end write, "Volcanic Vicki." At the other end write, "Restrained Robert." Explain to the children that the line is a self-control *continuum* and that Vicki and Robert represent the extreme endpoints. Ask the children to help you describe Vicki and Robert. Have fun with this and encourage the children to exaggerate their descriptions. For example:

Volcanic Vicki is going off all the time. At the slightest provocation, steam spews from her nostrils, tears from her eyes, and agonizing, earth shaking sounds from her throat. Vicki was once able to control herself for 20 seconds, and that was when a bee landed on her nose.

Restrained Robert looks a little like an automated store mannequin. His expression almost never changes and his movements are stiff and controlled. People have exhausted themselves trying to make Robert laugh, or blink, or get angry. But Robert would rather die than lose control.

Ask two or three children at a time to write their names somewhere on the continuum. Explain that before they do this, they must decide how much self-control they have. Are they closer to Vicki's end of the continuum or Robert's? Give all of the children an opportunity to place themselves on the line.

Lead a culminating group discussion, focusing on the concepts of self-control and self-management. Then, with the last few minutes remaining, play a little game with the children. Tell them to sit absolutely still, without fidgeting, talking, or blinking. Explain that the last child to move is the winner. Time the children and proclaim the winner, "Self-control King" or "Self-control Queen" for the day.

Discussion Questions:

1. Why is it important to learn self-control?
2. What would school be like if children and teachers never made any effort to manage their feelings or behavior?
3. What does self-management have to do with responsibility?
4. What do your parents mean when they tell you to "be on your best behavior?"
5. How do you feel when you successfully control yourself?

Variation:

Draw an imaginary self-control line on the floor and have the children stand in the spot that represents their place on the continuum. Have two children act out the parts of Volcanic Vicki and Restrained Robert while standing at either end of the imaginary line.

A Time I Felt Anger and Handled It Well

A Sharing Circle

Objectives:

The children will:
— verbally acknowledge themselves and others for successfully controlling anger.
— identify techniques for controlling anger.

Introduce the Topic:

Anger is one of the hardest emotions to deal with. It doesn't feel good and it's hard to control. In this session, we're going to talk about successfully controlling anger. Our topic is, "A Time I Felt Anger and Handled It Well."

Think of a time when you were angry at something or someone, but you bit your lip, or counted to ten, or did something else to keep from blowing up. You may have been mad at a friend, parent, teacher, brother or sister, and it could have been over something important or a tiny thing. Tell us what happened and what you did to control yourself, but please don't mention any names. The topic is, "A Time I Felt Anger and Handled It Well."

Discussion Questions:

1. Why is it important to control anger? What kinds of things can anger lead to if it isn't controlled?
2. What are some ways to let anger out, like air from a balloon, without actually getting angry?
3. What have you learned about anger from this session?

A Time I Accepted Someone Else's Anger

A Sharing Circle

Objectives:

The children will:
— describe ways of diffusing another person's anger.
— explain that to manage anger requires self-control.

Introduce the Topic:

Anger is a difficult emotion to handle when you feel it inside, and also when someone else's anger is coming directly at you. It's hard to just stand there and catch anger the way you do a softball. But we've all done it, and that's what were going to talk about today. Our topic is, "A Time I Accepted Someone Else's Anger."

Think about a time when someone was angry at you, and instead of being angry back, or getting defensive, you just accepted the anger. Like a baseball catcher, you let the anger come right at you and caught it, and because you were prepared to catch the anger, it didn't hurt so much. Maybe a parent was angry at you for something, and you accepted the anger. Or perhaps a friend was angry at you, but you knew it was mostly because your friend was in a bad mood, so you were patient and let it happen. Tell us the circumstances without mentioning any names, and describe how you stayed in control. The topic is, "A Time I Accepted Someone Else's Anger."

Discussion Questions:

1. Why is another person's anger so difficult to accept?
2. What is the first thing you want to do when someone is angry at you?
3. Why do you think it helps to just accept the other person's anger and not do anything back?
4. What have you learned about anger from this session? ...about self-control?

What Did You Learn About Self-Control?

Use this page to think about and record the things you have learned about self-control. You can write, draw pictures, scribble and doodle, create a poem, or anything else that has meaning to you and will help you remember what you have learned.

When you finish, show this page to someone else and explain what you have learned.

Tips for Teaching Self-Control:

♡ You are your child's most important teacher! Model the kind of behavior you hope to see your child display. If you are trying to teach self-control, but lash out angrily at your child when he misbehaves, he will learn to do as you do, not as you say.

———————

♡ Help your child to think about the consequences of his or her behavior. Remember to praise your child for doing things that demonstrate self-control.

———————

♡ Talk with your child about self-control. When you're watching television or in real life and you notice a person acting badly, comment to your child about what that person is doing, and how that behavior reflects a lack of self-control. Discuss what you see, and hear. Ask questions such as, "What could that person have done differently instead of...?"

Dear Parents,

We have been learning about self-control in our Hearts and Minds group. In our activities and Sharing Circles the children not only described examples of self-control and self-management but also demonstrated the behaviors associated with these skills. I encourage you to ask your child, "What does self-control mean?" and encourage your child to demonstrate those important skills

Our story this week is entitled An Alterna-Tive Tale. This story is about the Want family who lived in a very large house, which they needed. There were sixteen people in the family and they lived in a state of confusion. Everyone had his or her own thoughts and no one could agree on anything. They were always arguing. It was not a happy, respectful, kind, tolerant family at all! Until the family hired a household manager named Alterna-Tive, who got her name from the word alternative. Alterna showed the Wants new ways to work with each other.

There were lots of scenarios in the story that illustrated self-control. The children shared some awesome thoughts during our discussions. Ask your child to share some of the "do's" and "don'ts!" we talked about.

Happy sharing thoughts together...

PEER PRESSURE

— It is impossible to persuade a man who does not disagree, but smiles.

Muriel Spark

— Life shrinks or expands in proportion to one's courage.

Anais Nin

Vocabulary Words

- Gurgled
- Wobbled/wobbliness
- Cowardice
- (Juvenile) Delinquent
- Murmured
- Goad
- Dominated

Sweet Revenge

by Tom Pettepiece

"Dare you!" Morey said.

I gulped. Morey had dared me before to do things at school, like ten pull-ups on the high bar, or kick the girl's ball during recess. Once he even dared me to stick out my tongue at the teacher while she wasn't looking, which I did, though I could have sworn she saw me at the last minute when she turned her head and I yanked my tongue quickly into hiding.

Truth is, I was weary of Morey's dares, and today's felt worse than ever before. My stomach gurgled like an empty cavern. My legs felt rubbery — I wobbled like a Saturday morning cartoon character.

I was standing with Morey and three other boys right below Mr. Brickle's big picture window, where Mr. Brickle stood every day after school and watched us kids walk home. If he saw anyone goofing off, or bothering the girls, or — worst of all — stepping on his property in the slightest, on any part, the grass or the flower bed with tulip bulbs waiting for Spring, he'd pound on the window and shake his fist at us. And if that didn't work, he'd disappear from view for a moment, then reappear on the porch shouting, "You kids better stay out of my yard if you know what's good for you!" None of us ever really knew what wouldn't be good for us if we didn't, but we never had the courage to defy the old man and find out. Until now that is.

All eyes were on me, the growing silence giving away my cowardice in the face of pressure. I didn't know which was worse, the fear of Brickle or the fear of saying no to my friends.

"Come on, James," one of the guys urged. "Are you or aren't you?"

"Yeah. You're the one who's always talking so tough, saying 'Mr. Brickle is as dumb as a pickle,' and stuff like that. Are you going to throw that rock or not?"

I admit, I'd wanted to get even for a long time — ever since Brickle yelled at me for parking my bike on the sidewalk in front of his house while I ran after my dog. When I came back the bike was gone, and I didn't get it back for a week. My parents made me go over and apologize to Mr. Brickle, even though they agreed that I hadn't done anything wrong. The sidewalk *was* public property. Only problem was, Mr. Brickle or someone else walking by might have fallen trying to go around the bike blocking their way.

That same night after dinner, my buddies and I had met on the corner of Mr. Brickle's street and talked about getting even with the old man by breaking his precious picture window. Then he couldn't stand there and stare at us anymore. Morey was convinced that tonight was the perfect time, since on our way home from school we'd seen Mr. Brickle's son drive off with him. It was twilight, dark enough so we couldn't be seen from the street in the bushes beneath the window, but light enough for Morey to find the medium-sized rock he now held out to me.

"You're chicken, James," one of the guys said. "All talk and no action," said another.

"Well, you do it then, Big Mouth," I shot back.

"He didn't take *my* bike, man."

"Yeah, but he's yelled at you as much as me, calling you a punk kid and a juvenile delinquent."

The other boys murmured agreement. It was true. Brickle had insulted us all at one time or another. Not one kid who walked by his house had been spared the wrath of his cruel words. Hadn't Mr. Brickle ever been a kid? What was wrong with him anyway?

"Well, James?" they all echoed in unison. "It's getting dark. Let's go. Now or never."

"Okay, okay." I was starting to feel annoyed at the pressure. I figured they were just as scared as I was, that's why they were trying to goad me into doing it. Breaking someone's window was wrong — even the window of a mean old man like Brickle.

I decided to fake them out. "I'll do it on one condition," I said.

"What?" asked Morey.

"That we're all in this together. If anyone gets caught, we all get caught. And if anyone runs, the deal is off. Got it?"

They all looked at each other for a moment, then back at me.

"Okay. Do it."

I stepped back so I could see the front of the house, dominated by the window. It was an old wooden house, built over sixty years ago, with brick around the bottom. The section with the big window jutted out toward the street, so while it provided a perfect viewing stand for Mr. Brickle, it also made a perfect target.

I tossed the rock up and down in my palm, higher each time. I eyed the glass as though it were a bull's-eye on a shooting range. "Let's get Brickle, let's get Brickle," I began to chant. My arm was up in the air now, making circles as if I was preparing to throw the rock all the way to China. "Get Brickle, get Brickle, get Brickle."

"Quiet!" hissed Morey. "You want everyone in the neighborhood to hear you?"

Ignoring Morey's warning, I shouted, "Spread out guys, so you don't get hit by flying glass! Here I go... one, two..."

"RUN!" cried Morey as they all scattered like squirrels fleeing the hunter.

"Three!"

I held onto the rock for a moment before letting it drop harmlessly to the ground. I turned away just in time to see the other guys disappear around a corner.

Heading home, I noticed that the wobbliness in my legs was gone. I started to whistle a tune. "What'll Morey come up with next?" I wondered.

Discussion Questions:

1. What was the conflict James felt before he made his decision?
2. Did the fact that Mr. Brickle was a mean person make it all right to destroy his property? Why not?
3. Why didn't Morey throw the rock himself?
4. How else could the boys have handled their anger at Mr. Brickle?
5. Did James really want to break the window? How do you know?
6. What did the boys say and do to try to pressure James into throwing the rock?
7. What was James trying to accomplish by "faking out" Morey and the other boys?
8. What are some other ways that James could have resisted the pressure of his friends?
9. How do you think James felt as he headed home?

Sweet Revenge

Experience Sheet

Think about the story of James and his friends and how James handled the pressure the other boys put on him to do something he knew was wrong.

1. What would you have said and done if you were James?

2. Have you ever been pressured by other kids to do something wrong? What kinds of things did they say and do to pressure you?

3. How did you react to the pressure? Did you go along with them or did you resist in some way?

4. Why do kids sometimes do things they know are wrong just because other kids want them to?

Dozens of Ways to Say No

Brainstorming, Role Play and Discussion

Objectives:

The children will:
— distinguish between friendly and teasing forms of peer pressure.
— formulate and practice specific ways of saying no to peer pressure.

Materials:

chart paper or large sheets of butcher paper; markers or pens

Directions:

Have the children form groups of six to eight and choose a recorder. Give each group a sheet of chart or butcher paper.

Write the word, *friendly* on the board and draw a smiley face next to it. Remind the children that sometimes peer pressure comes in friendly forms — from kids they know and like. Perhaps the hardest thing about saying no to friendly pressure is the fear of hurting a relationship or losing a friend. But by saying no in a friendly way, the children can stand up for themselves while at the same time reassuring their friend that they like and value him or her. They may even influence their friend to say no, too. Offer some examples of friendly responses (see last page of activity).

Tell the groups to write down as many friendly ways of saying no as they can brainstorm in 5 minutes. Circulate among the groups, randomly role-playing sources of friendly pressure by saying to individual children (for example): *Oh, don't worry, Karen it's only a little glass of beer.*

Next, write the word *teasing* on the board and draw a smirky face next to it. Remind the children that dares, bribes, put downs and other forms of teasing are also used to pressure us to do things we shouldn't do. One of the hardest things about saying "no" to teasing pressure is not wanting to look foolish, dumb, or weak. Learning "snappy" ways to say no can help. Offer some examples of snappy responses (next page).

Ask the groups to write down as many snappy ways of saying no as they can brainstorm in 5 minutes. Encourage them to have fun. Circulate and role play sources of teasing pressure, e.g.: *Hey, grow up Dave — are you always going to do what your mommy says?*

Have the groups take turns reading their friendly and snappy responses to the group. Then post the lists where everyone can see them.

Practice using the responses. Randomly approach different children and role play peer pressure situations, such as offering them alcohol and other drugs, or goading them into unethical or illegal acts. Vary your invitations from friendly to teasing. Have the children pick their responses from the posted lists. Encourage them to stand, and to use appropriate posture, gestures, facial expressions, volume, etc.

Conclude the activity with a general group discussion.

Discussion Questions:

1. Why is it sometimes hard to say no to a friend?
2. If a friend gets mad at you when you say no, what can you do to feel better about it?
3. Why does it help to practice saying no in different ways?

Sample Friendly Responses

— No, I really don't want to.
— I'd like to go to your party, but if no adults are going to be there I can't.
— No thanks. Why don't we ride bikes instead?
— I don't want to mess up my mind, and I wish you wouldn't mess up yours either.
— No, I never put this body in dangerous situations. Let's think of something else to do.

Sample Snappy Responses

— No thanks, I'd rather walk my pet python.
— I'm not interested. I've got better things to do.
— No thanks. I like to get my bad breath from pepperoni pizza.
— Thanks, but if I'm going to ruin my body, I'll do it with a hot fudge sundae.
— No, but do you happen to have any milk? I'm on a program to build brain cells.

Four Ways to Say No!
Discussion and Skill Development

Objectives:

The children will:
— learn four ways of saying no.
— practice using refusal skills to resist peer pressure.

Materials:

chart paper and markers or whiteboard; a watch or clock with a second hand

Directions:

Remind the children of any previous discussions/activities related to peer pressure. Suggest that when they decide to resist peer pressure, the next big challenge is to say no. Saying no can be hard, particularly in the face of teasing, put-downs, promises, and threats.

Write these four methods of saying no on the board and discuss them with the children. Do a few quick role plays for practice.

1. Say no

    No, thank you.

    Say it politely, firmly, or any other way that fits the situation. If necessary, repeat it. Use the "broken record" technique.

2. Say no and give a reason.

No. I don't want to hurt my lungs.

Keep your explanation short. Remember, you have a right to make your own decision. You don't have to justify or defend yourself.

3. Say no and change the subject or suggest something else to do.

No thanks. Let's ride our bikes to the park.

Be assertive. Take charge of the situation. Do something you want to do.

4. Say no and leave.

No. (while walking away)

Use this method when the other three don't work. Always use this method with strangers or if you think you are in danger. Go immediately for help.

Point out that it pays to learn four different ways to say no because sometimes saying no once, or in just one way, doesn't work. Explain: *One reason saying no doesn't always work is that the person we are saying no to often doesn't accept our refusal. Instead, he or she keeps trying to convince us to do the thing we don't want to do. You've probably been in this sort of situation many times — trying to resist a brother, sister, or friend who pleads, argues, and tries to get you to change your mind.* Act out a familiar example, such as one child persistently urging another to come over to his or her house.

Ask the children to pair up and sit facing each other for a practice exercise. Have them decide who will be the Convincer and who will be the Resister in the first round. List several starter situations on chart paper or the board, such as:

— Try some of these pills.
— Go to the movie I want to see.
— Let me copy your homework.
— Take out the trash for me.

Coach the Convincers to try anything they can think of to get a "yes" answer. Tell the Resisters to keep resisting, using any or all of the four methods. The livelier this exercise gets, the better. Encourage enthusiastic role playing. Allow at least 1 minute for each round. Then have the children switch roles and pick a new topic from the list.

Conclude the activity with a group discussion.

Discussion Questions:

1. How did you feel as the Convincer?
2. How did you feel when you were saying no?
3. Which method of saying no was easiest for you? Which was hardest?
4. Did you feel like you had to explain your reasons for saying no?
5. Did resisting get any easier as you continued to do it?

A Group I Like Belonging To

A Sharing Circle

Objectives:

The children will:
— describe the dynamics of a group to which they belong.
— identify benefits of participating in a group of peers.

Introduce the Topic:

Our topic today concerns groups. It is, "A Group I Like Belonging To." Think of a group in which you enjoy participating. Maybe it's simply a group of friends, but it could also be a club or organization of some sort. For example, maybe you're a member of safety patrol, or scouts, or the band. Of perhaps you enjoy being part of an athletic team, a drama group, or child council. Tell us about the group you enjoy and how you became a part of that group. Our topic is, "A Group I Like Belonging To."

Discussion Questions:

1. How long has your group been together? What kinds of things do you do together?
2. Is your group open to new members? How does a person join?
3. How strong is the peer pressure in your group? Can individuals go against the majority without losing their place in the group?

A Time I Said No
A Sharing Circle

Objectives:

The children will:
— describe what it is like to say no to a friend.
— affirm one another for having and exercising refusal skills.

Introduce the Topic:

Our topic today is, "A Time I Said No." As you think about this topic, focus on times you have said no to your peers. Try to recall a situation in which a friend asked you to do something that you didn't want to do — or maybe you did want to do it but knew it was wrong. Perhaps a friend asked you to give him the answers on a test or let him copy your homework. Or maybe someone asked you to lie for her, and say that she was with you when she wasn't. Maybe a friend offered you a cigarette or alcohol. Whatever it was, you said no. Tell us what happened and how you felt when you refused, but please don't mention any names. The topic is, "A Time I Said No."

Discussion Questions:

1. What does it take to say no to a friend?
2. Is it possible to say no to a friend without losing that person's friendship? How?
3. Have you ever said yes while wishing you had the guts to say no? What would have happened if you had said no?

What Did You Learn About Peer Pressure?

Use this page to think about and record the things you have learned about peer pressure. You can write, draw pictures, scribble and doodle, create a poem, or anything else that has meaning to you and will help you remember what you have learned.

When you finish, show this page to someone else and explain what you have learned.

Tips for Teaching Kids How to Deal with Peer Pressure:

♡ It's important to know who your child's friends are and with whom he or she hangs out. Make sure you listen to what the kids say to each other so you can tell whether your child is associating with a safe circle of friends.

♡ Being a "best friend" to your child is a good way to deal with your child's growing interests in peers and the natural "wannabe" attitude. Be your child's best friend by sharing your own varied experiences as a child and how you coped with similar peer pressure.

♡ When you give your child opportunities to make his or her own choices, you are teaching problem solving and independence. Giving your child ways to express preferences and make decisions shows that his or her ideas and feelings matter. Your child's self-confidence deepens and leads to better decision making and less likelihood of being influenced by negative peer pressure.

Dear Parents,

In our Hearts and Minds group, we have been discovering ways of dealing with peer pressure and have practiced how to use refusal skills to resist that pressure. This is a very important skill to have in this day and age. Your child not only wrote about his or her personal experience with peer pressure, but also role-played with appropriate responses for saying "no." I encourage you to ask, "What did you learn today?" If he or she says "nothing", like kids sometimes do, let me give you a heads up as to what we did.

Today's story, Sweet Revenge, was about a group of boys who were pressuring a friend, James, to throw a rock through the picture window of the grumpy old man who lived on their street. The leader of the group, Morey, was always challenging people to do bad things. James was always the one on a dare. Throughout the story, James was feeling uneasy about the challenge because he knew it was wrong. Thinking of how to get out of it, James came up with a way to see if his "friends" were as tough as they thought. He was about to throw the rock and told his friends that they were all in it together and no one could run and hide. Even though Morey and the group agreed, their behavior showed differently. Everyone ran away on the count of two! James yelled three and put the rock back on the ground and walked away.

The children shared some great ways to say "no" to peer pressure. Ask about it. And I encourage you to ask your child to practice for you some of the friendly and snappy responses. You'll be helping your child reinforce these important behaviors for resisting peer pressure.

Happy talking together....

If your heart is in Social-Emotional
Learning, visit us online.

Come see us at
www.InnerchoicePublishing.com

Our web site gives you a look at all our other Social-Emotional Learning-based books, free activities, articles, research, and learning and teaching strategies. Every week you'll get a new Sharing Circle topic and lesson.

INNERCHOICE Publishing

15079 Oak Chase Court
Wellington, FL 33414

www.ingramcontent.com/pod-product-compliance
Lightning Source LLC
Chambersburg PA
CBHW081217230426
43666CB00015B/2774